How *to* Get Your Husband *to* Listen *to* You

Nancy Cobb
Connie Grigsby

How to Get Your Husband to Listen to You

MULTNOMAH
BOOKS

How to Get Your Husband to Listen to You
Published by Multnomah Books
12265 Oracle Boulevard, Suite 200
Colorado Springs, Colorado 80921
A division of Random House Inc.

ISBN 978-1-59052-742-9

Library of Congress Cataloging-in-Publication Data
Cobb, Nancy.
　　How to get your husband to listen to you / Nancy Cobb, Connie Grigsby. —
1st ed.
　　　　p. cm.
　　ISBN 978-1-59052-742-9
　1. Marriage—Religious aspects—Christianity.　2. Communication in marriage.
3. Listening—Religious aspects—Christianity.　4. Man-woman relationships—
Religious aspects—Christianity.　I. Grigsby, Connie.　II. Title.
　　BV835.C592 2008
　　248.8'435—dc22

　　　　　　　　　　　　　　　2007032462

Printed in the United States of America
2008—First Edition

10　9　8　7　6　5　4　3　2　1

Special Sales
Most WaterBrook Multnomah books are available in special quantity discounts when
purchased in bulk by corporations, organizations, and special interest groups. Custom
imprinting or excerpting can also be done to fit special needs. For information, please
e-mail SpecialMarkets@WaterBrookPress.com or call 1-800-603-7051.

CONTENTS

Introduction 1
Prologue 5

PART 1: WHY IS THIS SO HARD?

1. So He's Not Exactly Prince Charming? 11
2. Bride Sightings 18
3. Male-Speak 24
4. Talking: Direct Versus Indirect 30
5. Hinting Doesn't Work 38
6. Exactly What Language Are You Speaking? 41
7. Wired, Not Weird 45
8. His-and-Her Hormones 49
9. Conversational Goals 53
10. Rapport Versus Report 57

PART 2: HOW YOU SHOOT YOURSELF IN THE FOOT

11. Nagging 63
12. Nonverbal Communication and Love Languages 70
13. Jumping to Conclusions 74
14. The Ha-Ha's 77
15. Women Way Overthink 80
16. Don't Ask If You Don't Want an Answer 82
17. Who Influences You? 90

PART 3: OPENING HIS HEART OPENS HIS EARS

18. A Thankful Heart 101
19. Let Go of One Thing 106
20. Choose Discipline 115
21. A Marriage Thermometer 121
22. RECONNECTing 124
23. Circular Thinking 131
24. Giving Respect 134
25. What Your Disrespect Triggers 138
26. Two Ways to Spell Intimacy 144
27. Conflict Comes...but It Shouldn't Stay 146
28. A Gentle Response 155
29. Choose Words with Care 159
30. Cut to the Chase 165
31. You're Entitled! 167
32. He's Your Defender...and You're His 175

PART 4: AHA! MOMENTS

33. Guess Who Gave Him His Personality? 181
34. Maybe I'm Not as Right as I Thought I Was 185
35. The Next Time 193
36. Uncovering How Men Communicate 201
37. You Might Be Surprised 210
38. CPR for a Dying Marriage 217
39. It Won't Always Make Sense 220

Afterthoughts 223
Epilogue 225
Acknowledgments 232

INTRODUCTION

"YOU HAVE LESS THAN TWO WEEKS to live unless you have chemotherapy—and even with chemo, you have at the most nine to twelve months." How would you live your life if an oncologist said these words to you and your husband?

When my husband, Ray, and I (Nancy) heard this, we were dumbfounded…devastated.

Just two weeks earlier we'd seen our internist, and Ray had been diagnosed with shoulder strain. (We didn't know at the time that severe shoulder pain is one of the first signs of cancer.) But then one morning Ray was so out of breath he couldn't put on his socks and shoes to go to work.

Connie (coauthor of this book) is married to Wes Grigsby, a doctor who heads the emergency room of a local hospital. We went to see Wes, and Ray was admitted. The following day we discovered he had stage-four cancer of the lungs, liver, and kidneys.

For reasons beyond my understanding, the "lion" I married became a very silent man in the many meetings with medical personnel that followed. Incredibly, I, the quiet one, became the lion. Much to Ray's surprise, I—armed with my portfolio of all his medical records—became quite blunt when speaking to those who treated him.

Ray went into two remissions. Both times we flew east to visit our children.

As the months went by, Ray faced the facts, and we chose to live each day to the fullest.

One day he said, "We're in this together, in everything that happens, and I'm so glad. That's why I married you."

Near the end, he bought me a CD by country-western singer Alan Jackson called *Precious Memories*. Ray told me he was dedicating one of the songs on the album to me: "I Want to Stroll over Heaven with You." Then he asked something that still touches me to the core: "Nan, when you get to heaven, how will I find you?"

I reminded him that when there were five billion people on this earth, God had brought the two of us together for the first time in Fuchu, Japan. He could surely bring us together again when that day came.

Then I shared the most important question I'd ever asked him…and Ray *listened*. I asked if he was sure he was going to heaven.

He replied that he wasn't.

I shared the gospel with him: he needed to admit he'd sinned, acknowledge that Jesus died on the cross for his sins, and be willing to turn from his sins and ask Him to come and dwell within him in the presence of the Holy Spirit.

I asked Ray if he believed what I'd said. He replied that he did. I then asked if I could pray with him, and he told me I could.

That same week, Connie and I finished this book.

And Ray died.

Because of the grace of God and because Ray was willing to listen to me, I know that he is now in heaven.

I mourned greatly for weeks. Then a great peace came over me. For some reason, experiencing that peace made me feel guilty. I shared this with my sister, Christine, who told me, "Nan, peace is the laurel wreath that God gave you for finishing the race well."

I now know that the peace I feel is a gift from God. My husband listened to me because he loved me. I had literally studied Ray for years so we could communicate. I adapted to his style of communication. And the payoff was divine.

Does your husband listen to you? He will...if you understand the way your husband communicates and accept him the way God created him. Then—and only then—will he listen to you.

It could be that eternity hangs in the balance.

PROLOGUE

EVERY MORNING RAY AND I (NANCY) come downstairs to enjoy a cup of coffee and read the paper together. I read the Life section first, solve word puzzles, look at the television guide, and read some of the cartoon strips. As the morning progresses, we switch sections.

I recently read a cartoon where a dad is talking to his son about how to impress women. The father tells him that he needs to ask women questions about what interests them and then listen very carefully to the answers. After a long pause, the son replies with amazement that this crazy approach might just work.

This week I went to a well-known bookstore that has twelve hundred branches throughout the world, thirty-five thousand employees, and a customer base of thirty million. I was using its computer to locate material on the way men's brains are wired for listening. Halfway through my search, a young man who

worked there asked if he could help me. I told him I was looking for a book I thought was titled *Men Don't Listen Well*.

He stared blankly, then said after a moment, "I'm sorry. I
forgot what you said. What did you say?"

I couldn't stop laughing. Without even a smile on his face,
he asked me again to tell him the title of the book—which made
me laugh even more.

Perhaps, as a wife, you sometimes feel like the hitchhiker in
this story:

Sally was driving home from one of her business trips in
northern Arizona when she saw an elderly Navajo woman walking on the side of the road. Since the trip was a long and quiet
one, she stopped the car and asked the woman if she would like
a ride. With a silent nod of thanks, the woman got into the car.

Resuming the journey, Sally tried in vain to make a bit of
small talk with the woman. The old woman just sat in silence,
looking intently at everything she saw, studying every little
detail, until she noticed a white bag on the seat next to Sally.
"What is in the bag?" the old woman asked.

Sally looked down at the white bag and said, "It's a box of
chocolates. I got it for my husband."

The woman was silent for another moment or two. Then
speaking with the quiet wisdom of an elder, she said, "Good
trade."

Many of us have had those days when such a trade might
seem at least slightly tempting. But there's something far better,

and that is becoming what God intended us to be within the marriage relationship. Trading our old habits for godly ones is always a good trade.

We're assuming—because you've picked up this book—that your own communication process with your husband could benefit from some improved relational tools. It's our goal to provide you with those tools. Understanding your husband's brain in all his strengths and diversity also helps you to not take it personally when you two get your conversational and emotional wires crossed.

Between us, we've been married for seventy-five years. We're still learning, and we only wish we'd been more eager to learn in our early years (rather than trying to instruct our husbands on how they should change). One thing we've learned over the years is that change is always just a decision away. And we wish we'd made the decision much earlier to better understand our husbands.

We hope you won't wait as long as we did. We hope you'll begin soon—as in *today.*

If you're willing to learn, we believe this book will change not only you as a wife, but the entire landscape of your life as well. Yes, that's a tall promise. But we've come to see that tall promises have a way of coming true when God is involved.

PART I

WHY IS THIS SO HARD?

1

SO HE'S NOT EXACTLY PRINCE CHARMING?

IS ANYONE OUT THERE NOT FAMILIAR with the story of Cinderella? As little girls, we were sure our prince would some-day come.

Have you ever considered that your husband, as a dewy-eyed little boy, heard the same fairy tale and likewise expected to find you, his Cinderella? to be a prince for you—to slay your dragons, to provide you with a castle, and to live happily ever after? to be your knight in shining armor?

Husbands are often painfully aware that we tend to see them not as our Prince Charming but as the frog we have to kiss, hoping that he will, at long last, be transformed into that prince. *And he can't understand it.* We appeared to be so happy with him when he slipped the ring on our finger. Is it just a coincidence that on our wedding day, as we wore a lovely dress and were attended by handmaidens, we appeared to be Cinderella at the ball?

What happened? Why has the magic dust lost its luster?

We sort of know, don't we? But we prefer not to tell him. We want him to figure it out and do princely, romantic things again and continue to sweep us off our feet. And he—as best he can and in his direct manner—tries to do just that:

Husband: "What's wrong? Did I do something?"

Wife: "Nothing's wrong. Everything is just fine."

Husband: "Well, you're acting like you're upset with me."

Wife: "Why would I be upset with you?"

At this point your husband gives up and goes back to reading the paper.

When women say, "Men can't communicate," what we really mean is, "Men can't communicate the way women communicate." And to a man, it seems that women can't communicate at all.

Recently we were talking about some of our favorite authors with a group of friends. Most everyone liked Hemingway, but someone shared their viewpoint that he seemed to struggle when writing dialogue for his female characters. He seemed unable to get inside a woman's head. And he was neither the first nor the last.

A TV episode of *Seinfeld* offers a more recent example. Jerry and his friend George are trying to write a pilot for a comedy show. They wrestle over having the right dialogue to flow from the mind of their female character. Utterly at a loss, they finally cut her out of the script entirely.

In novels, on television, and in real life, what and how a woman thinks is truly a mystery to men, even brilliant men. A woman's thought process is baffling to most of our male counterparts. And one aspect of that mystery is the frequent perception that men are the villains, though the nature of their offenses is fuzzy. The mystery of how a woman thinks makes little sense to men, and we offer few clues to aid in the deciphering. Eventually the mystery of a woman's thoughts becomes just too much trouble for a man to figure out.

As women, we likewise become frustrated by the difficulties we have communicating with our husbands. Since most men are able to exchange information in a logical, direct, and efficient manner, how is it possible we women have such a hard time interacting with them?

Male communication is no frills, while female communication is fraught with frills. We often want our men to listen to us the way our mothers, sisters, and girlfriends listen to us. The problem is that while men have no trouble relating to other men, they have a huge problem relating to women, because they aren't doing what women think they should do. We tend to see their efforts as far too blunt and direct, even rude.

To flip the complaint of Henry Higgins in *My Fair Lady:* "Why can't a man be more like a woman?" There's a simple answer: men don't *want* to be more like women. They're born male, and they're hard-wired to grow into men. Trying to get them to interact as we do will never work. Such behavior would be completely unnatural and foreign to them.

Consider, for instance, our female way of not saying what we really mean. That is one of the things that bothers men most about women. It forces men to strain every cell in their brains to listen in hopes of both uncovering what we're *really* saying and responding somewhere in the ballpark with the answers we want.

Our tendency to not say what we really mean points to our biggest communication problem. Do you know what it is? *The truth.*

For example, we come downstairs wearing new pants and ask, "How do I look?" (That's code for, "I'm hoping for a compliment.") The only time we really want the truth is *before* we buy the pants, and even then it has to be handled correctly (with words like, "The other pair looks even better").

But no husband knows this. We haven't given him a copy of the playbook. He listens to our words, thinks we're asking a simple, straightforward question, and then gives a simple, straightforward answer: "Well, I think they make your bottom look huge."

This is not a good answer. Who cares if it's the truth or not? (Certainly not us!) At the very least he could have said "rather large" instead of "huge."

Now under the glare of your annoyance, Hubby is not too sure where he went wrong. After all:

- He listened.
- You asked his opinion.
- He evaluated your appearance—as requested.
- The pants don't flatter your body shape.
- He thought you wanted the truth.
- He attempted to give it to you.
- And now he's in trouble.

He starts to realize that he violated some unspoken rule, but he has no idea which one. Do you see that he's not at fault here? We are. So here are some suggested remedies for this all-too-familiar scenario:

- If you don't want the truth, don't ask your husband's opinion.
- Decide to become more "user friendly" when you hear the truth.
- Recognize that what your husband—who loves you— tells you is probably what others will be thinking as well.
- Realize that he's actually trying to slay a dragon for you (the dragon being, in this case, unflattering pants).

Don't expect your husband to answer you in girl-speak or sister-talk. Husbands will embrace this language skill at about the same time they begin wearing lace doilies on their heads.

Such language is a waste of time to him. He wants to listen to what you have to say, then communicate back to you what he thinks. Otherwise, why talk? And why listen?

Let's return to the story of Cinderella and Prince Charming. Both you and your husband probably got something a little different from what you expected. Life isn't a fairy tale. The beautiful white dress has been packed away (or was lost three moves ago). The glass slippers have been replaced by sneakers. The white horse isn't paid off yet, and the castle has a pretty steep mortgage. You don't always understand each other, and you sometimes find each other annoying. Sometimes you hurt each other's feelings. And one of you may be trying harder than the other to make your life together work.

But when the dragon's at the door, your husband still wants to be the one to slay it for you, and if you can bring yourself to the point of accepting his flaws, he'll be oh so eager to overlook yours and listen to what you have to say.

Illustrating that truth is a poignant scene from the movie *On Golden Pond* when the aging wife, played by Katharine Hepburn, is comforting her husband, played by Henry Fonda. He has just found his way home after being lost during a walk in the woods. He feels extremely vulnerable and frightened. She tenderly cradles his head to her chest and reassures him tearfully, "You're my knight in shining armor."

This line brings a lump to a man's throat. It expresses all that our husbands want to be for us. This is what it boils down to for them—if we would only cooperate in allowing them to reach this goal.

If at some point in your marriage your husband gets lost in the woods of life, with all its snares and pitfalls, and, all scared and worried, somehow finds his way home again, what will you say to him? "You idiot! How could you have gotten lost?" Or, "You're so brave. You're so courageous. You're so wonderful! And you're still my knight in shining armor. Nothing can change that!"

How long has it been since you assured your husband he's still your knight? If it's been a while, why not make a decision to change that today?

BOTTOM LINE

A husband whose wife considers him a knight in shining armor is a far better listener than one who's considered otherwise.

BRIDE SIGHTINGS

SEVERAL YEARS AGO, WHEN I (CONNIE) was first trying to get a handle on this "wife" business, I went into the bathroom after a heated discussion with my husband. As I passed by the mirror, I caught a glimpse of myself. *Who are you?* I silently asked the woman peering back at me.

Of course I knew who she was. But I found myself wishing she were someone else. I didn't like what I saw. My forehead was wrinkled; my brow, creased; my jaw, clenched. I looked so unhappy.

Unhappy? I was flat-out miserable.

What on earth had happened to the young bride who had practically floated down the aisle years before, sheer rapture emanating from ever pore of her body as she drew near to her groom? She'd always dreamed of this moment, and there, at the end of the aisle, stood her Prince Charming—the most wonderful man on earth. Now, years later, Cinderella was so sour.

I'm sure Prince Charming—who now stood alone in the kitchen while his princess assessed herself in the mirror—was wondering the same thing.

I'll tell you what happened. She started thinking she was doing more than her fair share of the relationship work, and she decided it was Prince Charming's turn to kick it up a notch or two. Prince Charming, however, was clueless about his bride's mind-set. He would have been shocked to hear she thought he hadn't been doing his part.

This scenario is all too common in marriages, young and old. Just this week we heard about some dear friends who are divorcing after twenty-six years because, according to the wife, "He simply doesn't do his part." She is tired of paddling upstream in the Relationship River with only one oar. Her husband is now in a place he never dreamed he'd be—and lost as to how he got there.

One of the interesting things we discovered while researching this book is that many men tend to think their marriages are way better than their wives would say. One reason for these conflicting perspectives is the vast difference in how men and women view "relationship work." After talking with dozens of women, we noticed a pattern: A couple marries, and all is well. Shortly thereafter, because a guy is task oriented, he'll frequently (and often unconsciously) view the "task" of finding the right woman to spend his life with as finished, and he moves on to other things. In no way does he feel he's neglecting his wife.

When she finally bares her soul and tells him she feels neglected, he's usually completely surprised.

The wife enters marriage thinking not only that he will continue his attentive behavior but that the attention will actually increase. After all, now she's his wife, and in her mind that's a higher calling than girlfriend or fiancée. But this usually doesn't happen. Hubby is thinking he can relax a bit. He married her, didn't he? What more could she want? Unless otherwise notified, he considers the relationship on firm footing. So he's kicking back at the same time she thinks he'll be ratcheting up. It's a recipe for disaster.

This behavior continues for a long while. The new bride so wants a happy marriage that, early on, she doesn't speak up and share these feelings with her groom. Not wanting to come across as needy, she frequently stuffs her thoughts and nurtures the hope that one day soon his attentiveness will return more fully.

Typically, the groom is unaware of his bride's deep need for emotional connection because he himself doesn't have that same deep need. If he's thinking about revving up anything, it's usually the physical relationship, not the emotional one. Enter another recipe for disaster.

Finally, after some time, the wife voices her frustration. She starts softly, but as she begins realizing how completely in the dark he is, her voice rises along with her anger. She is not happy.

This couple—like countless others—is experiencing the

sharp learning curve in discovering the vast differences between them. They once thought they had almost everything in common. Now they're wondering if they feel the same way about anything.

One of the biggest contributors to the tension is that men are, by and large, task oriented. Their way of loving their wives is by doing things: going to work, mowing the lawn, picking up groceries. For most women, these things are great, but they have little to do with a man's contribution to the relationship.

So a guy may well get out of bed five days a week, work eight- or ten-hour days, and come home Friday night feeling he's doing great in the Relationship Department. If he's worked especially hard during the week *and* coached a Little League baseball game or two *and* taken his daughter to ballet practice, he's feeling *really* good about things. Throw in the night he helped clean up the kitchen, and he's confident he's the world's best husband. Yet his wife seems a bit aloof, even irritated, and seems to want something more from him.

What more could she want? he wonders.

Plenty! She wants him to occasionally hold her without any expectations of physical intimacy. She wants him to call her from time to time to see what she's doing and to say he's thinking about her. She wants him to plan a romantic evening. She wants him to take her on a walk or a drive or to just sit out on the patio and talk, like they used to. She wants to go to coffee with him and have him reach over and touch her hand while he reads the sports page.

She wants him to woo her again. She wants to feel special again. She wants to be reminded *he can't live without her*—and to know he really believes that. She wants him to leave her a note on her pillow, the kitchen counter, or even on the pile of dirty laundry—anywhere—just once. She wants him to look into her eyes and tell her he loves her. She wants a "moment."

There are also things she *doesn't* want. She doesn't want him to pop her on the bottom with a dirty T-shirt as he passes through the kitchen. She doesn't want him punching her in the arm to let her know he loves her. Nor does she want to sit with him and watch football games all weekend long and hear him say it counts as quality time. She doesn't want to hear "Luv ya, babe" in place of "I love you, baby"—and she wants him to understand the difference.

At some moment in time, she points these things out. To him, she's simply splitting hairs. Again. He feels that no matter how hard he tries, he just can't win. She, however, feels he's hardly trying. And round and round they go. He wonders why she can't just relax and enjoy their great relationship. She's thinking there is no "great" in their relationship.

If that scenario is too much like your marriage, don't despair. It happens to almost everyone we know—certainly it happened to us. But the great news is that you don't have to live like this any longer. You can stop being mad at your husband and actually learn how to get inside his mind and start understanding how he thinks.

Best of all, you can get back to being you. The following pages will help you do just that.

BOTTOM LINE

*Your husband wants to listen
to the you that he married.*

Male-Speak

Isn't science amazing? Almost any problem (if analyzed closely enough) has a solution. So let's see how science can help with relational challenges.

As you travel through this book, you'll come across chapters on the differences between the male brain and the female brain. Because they're so vastly dissimilar, one can only imagine the wide gulf between men and women, producing what can only be called a disengaged relationship. Neither gender can understand the other…which can lead to neither one caring what the other says, understands, or feels. That's what prompts statements like these: "Oh, never mind." "Tell me one thing I just said." "No, *nothing* is wrong." And, "You told me that same story a year ago."

If, however, you begin to understand and converse in "male-speak," you'll not only bridge the gap, but you'll rally your guy. He'll begin listening more attentively to you, *and* you'll find he'll actually enjoy conversing with you.

Maybe you're mumbling to yourself, "I just don't understand why *I* have to do all the adjusting in our marriage… What about *him?*" There's a reason—a God-given reason. Generally speaking, women have been created to be more relational, whereas men have been created to be work focused. You probably know, for instance, that you can multitask better than your husband can. You probably think your way is better than your husband's. Your husband, however, is wired to concentrate on the task before him and see it through to completion—and he probably thinks his way is better than yours.

At times a woman may leave the bed half-made because the phone will ring, and after going to the kitchen to answer it, she'll unload the dishwasher while she's talking. Her husband (upon seeing the half-made bed) will call out, "Why are the pillows on the floor? Why do you leave things half-done? Why don't you finish something once you start it?" It's truly a puzzle to him.

This morning Ray and I were listening to the news. I was telling him about something; he was actually listening, and conversation ensued. Then the news switched to sports, and instead of giving me his full attention, he turned toward the TV, shushing me with a hand wave. I waited until the report was finished. Then, having completely forgotten I hadn't finished my story, he simply picked up the morning paper and began to read. Instead of being annoyed, I felt I was learning more and more about men's communication habits. For one thing, their attention span is *definitely* different from ours.

One more tip. If you want your husband to listen to you, don't interrupt him. In his male work environment, this would be seen as aggression or an attempt to control him, and he may respond to your interruptions from this mind-set. That's why a man's conversational tone switches from friendliness to annoyance when a woman interrupts him. His facial expression may not change, but his tone of voice will. He feels he isn't being respected, and this can result in his shutting down midsentence. He may totally stop listening to you, as though he's taken out a nonexistent hearing aid and become completely deaf.

Another complicating factor is that so often we women tell never-ending stories with pointless details. For example, here's a sentence a man can easily hear: "Mother and I went shopping today." But here's how it probably comes out in female-speak: "Mother and I went shopping today, and so when we couldn't find a parking place we went to another mall, and we didn't get to the store she really likes, and she didn't seem to have a good time, and so I took her to her favorite ice cream place and would you believe they didn't have chocolate swirl ice cream, the one she always orders, and so we went home, and do you want to hear what happened next that really shocked me?"

At this point, your husband just wants out of the room, away from the conversation—and from you as well. If you just wouldn't "and so" him to death, he probably would easily offer a comment after only a few words from you, especially if he could help solve some problem.

Yes, men are problem solvers. They passionately hate venting (unless it's their own). Meanwhile, most wives want to find a listening ear and then go on and on about a problem that their husbands could solve with a few words—and they would *love* to! So try a condensed approach to what you say: two sentences that end with a period. "I had an interesting day today, honey. I called the plumber, and he fixed the leaky faucet." This kind of talk is something your husband can get his head around. But he simply isn't wired to do the endless "and so" conversations.

If you tend to be long winded, you have a 75 percent chance of being interrupted. If your husband isn't the interrupting kind, then you have a 90 percent chance of simply being tuned out.

My (Nancy's) husband once pointed the TV remote at me and started clicking it. After a second he realized what he was doing, and we both started laughing. When I asked him what he was trying to do, he said, "I think I was trying to turn you off." (He's nothing if not honest!)

At other times, I think Ray would like to fast-forward me to get to more interesting content. If you're like me, this can hurt your feelings. But he's simply hurrying you along so he can fix whatever's bothering you. When you tell a man, "I don't want you to solve anything; I just want you to listen," then he thinks, *What's the point? I thought we were going to have a conversation. Don't conversations go something like, she says, I say, she responds, I respond—and then the verbal exchange is over?*

I think if someone could invent remotes with people silencers, husbands would very possibly camp out in the parking lot the night before they became available at Radio Shack.

Think about the last time you visited a male doctor. After examining you, he probably spoke briefly—maybe twenty-three seconds or so—and then started backing toward the door. I know about this, so I recently accompanied an older friend of mine to see her doctor. She had a few questions for him. He started backing up, but I was leaning against the door. She asked her questions, and he answered them. Only then did I slowly move away from the door (much to his relief, I'm sure).

Men, on the other hand, usually have no questions for their doctors. They think of themselves as a fine car being inspected by an expert mechanic. When these two task-oriented people meet, the mechanic listens to the client's engine and resets the timing as needed. Simple as that.

Men like short, direct conversation. They like a subject, a verb, and maybe an adjective or two. This is the form of conversation they're much more inclined to listen to *and* respond to—especially if, between thoughts, you leave moments of silence conducive to responses.

Also, never start a conversation with words such as, "We need to talk," or, "I have some issues I want to discuss with you." Openers like these are almost guaranteed to engender a husband's "Oh no! What is it now?" response.

I (Nancy) recently started a conversation that way with Ray. I just wanted to see his response. I knew it would be not only visible, but *clearly* visible—and it was. His brow furrowed, his lips went way up toward his nose, his nose was rising to his forehead, and frown marks were everywhere. When I told him I was simply teasing, the change in his body language was immediate. But he didn't laugh. He simply tried to regain his composure.

We women often think our way of speaking is more fun. It's not for a guy. And that's what your husband is.

BOTTOM LINE

A first step in getting your husband to listen to you is learning how to talk to him.

4

Talking: Direct Versus Indirect

When you're having a conversation with your husband, remember he's not a mind reader. So say what you mean.

If, for instance, you're on a drive together and you get thirsty, say, "Honey, would you please stop at the next Quick Shop? I'd like a soft drink." That's so much better than saying, "I'm so tired," and hoping he understands you're thirsty. He won't. If you're thirsty, say that you're thirsty. Otherwise the possibility will never enter his mind. Just say it!

This simple lesson took us wives years to learn—and that fact seems ridiculous to us now. Ray and Wes must have been completely exhausted wondering what they were supposed to be hearing when we wouldn't just come out and say it. Men tend to say exactly what they mean, while we women often beat around the bush or give hints.

In other words, men like Direct Talk. Women have a tendency to use Indirect Talk.

This fact was brought home to me (Connie) just a few months ago. My daughter Cassidy decided to train for a half marathon. She asked her dad and me if we'd like to train with her. I've been a runner for years, but I told her my arthritic knees weren't up for a thirteen-mile effort. Wes told her he was up for the challenge even though he hadn't run in a long while. He and Cassidy found a training schedule on the Internet and started training.

About a week into it, they asked if I'd like to run with them that evening, since they were going only a few miles and knew this was a distance I regularly ran. "Hmm," I said, thinking aloud. "That sounds kind of fun. Maybe I will. Or maybe it would be better if I didn't…"

I wanted to know if they *really* wanted me along, knowing I could slow them down. However, I hated to ask directly, so I used Indirect Talk, hoping they would get my signal.

Wes didn't pick up on it at all. He thought I simply couldn't decide. He had no idea I was fishing for reassurance.

"It doesn't really matter whether you're with us or not," he said. "We'll run the same distance. We need to get going, though. So you need to make up your mind."

This wasn't the response I was looking for, and my daughter knew it. Being female, she'd almost instantly translated my Indirect Talk. The moment Wes finished speaking, she jumped in:

"Oh, Mom, I think you should come. It'll be fun! And the three of us haven't run together in a long time."

"But what if I slow you down?"

I could see Cassidy's mouth forming words to reassure me, but before she got them out, Wes said, "That's a really good point. Since we're trying to make a certain time, and you can't really decide anyway whether to come"—which was, after all, what I'd originally said—"why don't you just stay here?"

He's Direct Talk all the way. He says what he means and doesn't beat around the bush. He can't really imagine, even after twentysome years of being married to Mrs. Indirect Talk, that a woman would do anything else.

At this point I could have felt hurt or sad, or pouted, or done one of many things along those lines (many, *many* things along those lines). But I'd gone down that path way too often, and I knew it was a complete waste of time and energy. In the past, I might have said, "Gee, Wes, I just wanted you to say how much you wanted me to come."

He would have answered, "Well, if we hadn't wanted you to come, we wouldn't have asked in the first place."

That kind of reasoning makes sense to me now. Most of the time. However, for twenty years it didn't. Back then, I thought Wes wasn't sensitive enough. I didn't realize we were speaking two different languages. The misconnection wasn't anyone's fault. It just was what it was. And it is still what it is.

With this hard-earned lesson in mind, I told Wes and Cass to go ahead, and I'd stay home and get some chores done while they were gone.

Before Cass could open her mouth to ask me to reconsider, Wes hustled her out the door. I could hear them speaking on the front porch as they did a few quick stretches.

"You know, Dad," Cass was saying to Wes, "Mom really wanted to come."

"What are you talking about?" Wes said, completely taken aback. "She said she didn't really care. If she'd wanted to come, she would have said so."

"No, Dad. What she was really saying was, 'Do you *really* want me to come or are you just being nice by asking?'"

"That's ridiculous," Wes said. "I'm 100 percent sure you're wrong. What would make you think such a thing anyway?"

"I'm a girl, Dad."

Wes was baffled, and he probably wondered if Cassidy was joking. Regardless, he had no interest in hearing more about it, especially when his mind was on running. So off they went, and I have no doubt he didn't give our conversation a second thought. In his mind, it was over.

Today, even after many years of marriage, we can still find ourselves sometimes thinking that one day Ray and Wes will finally "get" our Indirect Talk. But they probably won't. So over the years, we've chosen to change our goals. Rather than waiting on them to grasp our language, we're committed to understanding their Direct Talk and to not hold it against them when they say what they think.

Men aren't wired to decipher Indirect Talk. A woman can spend the better part of her marriage trying to teach it to her husband, but her efforts are, by and large, fruitless. Learning to speak his language is a far better investment of your time. Say what you mean and ask specifically for what you want—and do so with a minimum of words.

You'll be surprised at how freeing this is to both you and your husband. You'll also see what a waste of time it can be to wrap your words with hints, inferences, sighs, and nonverbal communication.

Even when you begin speaking Direct Talk, your husband might still need to be reminded of how you feel from time to time. This is because what you feel is the polar opposite of how he would feel in the same situation. In other words, don't expect to say something directly just once and think that whatever you've said is permanently embedded in his brain.

Here's an example. Not long ago we were at dinner with a couple we've known for years. This topic of Direct Talk came up. Lori said she likes John to hold her hand whenever they take a walk in the evenings, but she has to repeatedly ask him to do so.

John readily acknowledged to us that Lori had asked for this—and had used Direct Talk. His problem, he said, is that he forgets. It's on his mind the moment they're talking about it, but minutes later, when they head out for a walk, it's gone.

Lori turned to John in frustration. "Every time we go on a walk, do I have to tell you again that I'd like you to hold my hand?"

"Well," John replied, "if you want me to hold it, you do." Then he said in complete sincerity, "I know it doesn't make sense to you, but when we go on a walk, I'm not thinking about holding your hand, even though we've talked about it just moments before. I get outside and start thinking about whether or not there are grub worms in the lawn. Or I start looking at the driveway and wonder how that new crack got there. And as we walk past the neighbor's house, I'm wondering why they never shut their garage door or why his tomato plants are so much healthier than mine. Stuff like that. Holding your hand isn't anywhere near my radar screen."

"But if you loved me," Lori said, "you'd remember."

"It has nothing to do with loving you," John replied, shocked to hear her make such a connection. "If you'll just remind me or—better yet—just reach out and take my hand in yours, I promise to hold it for the rest of the walk. I want to make you happy and I want you to feel loved, but I really need you to help me on that."

This story probably grates a bit on your nerves. You hear John's words and think, *Clueless!* or something similar.

But it is what it is. The man needs reminding. Over and over and over again.

Women tend to think we shouldn't have to help our husbands by reminding them of what we like and want. We think that if they loved us, they should remember to do the things we ask them to do that make us feel special. But the short version of a very long answer is that most men don't remember.

They need our help. Not our nagging help, but warm, cooperative help. Help that refuses to take their forgetfulness personally, but instead is willing to step in and make them feel successful as husbands. We're knighting them, once again, when we help them in this way.

When we spoke with men about this topic, most of them readily admitted their need for their wives' help, but nearly all of them said they either didn't know how to ask for the help or were afraid that if they did ask, their wives would become even more frustrated by what they would perceive as ineptness.

It's been our experience, in talking with men, that most of them do as well as they know how to in this area. While we gals might roll our eyes and think they have to be joking, they're not. They just don't think or speak or act or remember like women do.

If you can grasp this, you're on your way to experiencing huge changes in your marriage…and to warming up your husband to want to listen to you.

Remember:

- Use Direct Talk.
- Don't take it personally if your husband forgets to do something you've asked him to do.
- Use "warm help" instead of nagging to set him up to succeed with your requests, especially if they involve affection.

BOTTOM LINE

*Men are better listeners when they're
not feeling they're in the doghouse.*

Hinting Doesn't Work

HINTING IS PERHAPS THE MOST common form of Indirect Talk. Your husband doesn't like hints unless they have to do with a surprise you're planning for him. He isn't a mind reader, and what your girlfriends or daughters instantly understand, he doesn't—unless you say it straight out.

Consider these two approaches you could take with your husband:

- "I can't believe how long it's been since we've had a romantic evening out together. Plus I've been so blue lately. I just can't seem to get myself out of this funk. Did you know Bob takes Julie out every Thursday night? Sometimes he even gets the baby-sitter himself."

- "You know what I'd like, darling? I'd like for the two of us to go out for dinner on Thursday night. I've been so blue lately, and I think a night out with you would lift my spirits immensely. Does Thursday night work for you?"

The difference is obvious. The first approach involves Indirect Talk, while the second is very direct. Men understand Direct Talk, and they like it when women clearly say what they want. It makes men feel safe. Indirect Talk makes them feel like they're being presented with a coded message that needs to be deciphered. It's wearisome and, in their minds, a total waste of time. Why would people talk in riddles when they could just say what they mean and be done with it?

Also, a man won't understand why—as in the first approach—we need to bring Bob and Julie into the equation. Even if he gets it, he'll resent being compared to Bob. Your husband wants you to admire *him,* not Bob. Men are competitive creatures, but they'll rarely feel the urge to compete with someone when you're the one pointing out the disparity. In fact, your doing so will cause your husband to resent you and usually cause him to resist doing whatever you're asking him to do. Why? Because he refuses to be manipulated by what he considers passive-aggressive behavior. Mentioning what another man does for his wife is *never* a good way to open communication channels with your husband.

It's reassuring to a man when his wife says exactly what she means. He'll feel that he's in safe waters where he doesn't have to worry about whether you're trying to convey something he's not getting. That's nerve racking for a guy.

As your husband starts hearing Direct Talk from you rather than convoluted hints, he'll begin to listen to you more. He'll no longer dread what you have to say.

Wes once said to me that my Indirect Talk made him feel like he was dodging bullets in an open field. He never knew when he was going to get hit.

Dodging bullets isn't fun for anyone, and it certainly doesn't open the door to talking and listening in a marriage.

BOTTOM LINE

*A husband who's busy dodging bullets
has little energy left to listen to you.*

6

Exactly What Language Are You Speaking?

Not long ago my (Nancy's) son Paul was teaching a study on the book of Genesis and gleaned great insight from his research. While preparing to teach about the Tower of Babel and the occasion when God confused the languages of the people, he shared something with me that I thought was inspired. Paul said this: "The confusion of language continues to the present day, especially between people speaking the same native language."

You see, neither you nor your husband really understands that you're speaking two different languages. Put simply, men are speaking content, but we women are responding to that content through all kinds of filters—body language, facial expression, tone of voice, and even our past relationship history.

Can you actually listen to and decode your husband's explanation of why he needs to buy a new car every year? Or why he would invite sixteen people to dinner the day you return from visiting your parents?

The differences between male-speak and female-speak can be noticed from early childhood. Consider that when a little girl is given a doll, it often becomes very real to her. She'll name it and begin to mother it, and this mothering will usually include such verbal affirmation as talking sweetly and singing lullabies.

On the other hand, when a young boy is given a doll, he sees it as an object and wants to know how it's put together. He's especially interested in what makes its eyes close, and he'll often pull them out for closer inspection.

We therefore weren't all that surprised to recently read an account of a woman psychologist who wanted to avoid any sexual stereotyping in her daughter's toys, thinking that the effort would help her little girl be more successful in a male-dominated culture. This woman gave her daughter a truck to encourage a more empowered self-image. But when the psychologist peeked in on her daughter at play, she saw that the girl had wrapped her truck in a blanket. She was rocking it tenderly and, in her most comforting voice, saying, "Don't worry, little truckie. Everything will be all right."

How are these traits established so early in life?

Although such male-female differences are noticeable in early childhood, the scientific basis of the difference goes back even further. Genetic components necessary for sexual development are actually present at the point of fertilization. Females have two X chromosomes, and males have an X and a Y chromosome. If a Y chromosome is present, then early in fetal development a testosterone bath occurs in utero and causes sexual differentiation into maleness. If this testosterone bath didn't occur, all babies would be female.

Researchers at Cambridge University have further documented the early onset of male and female differences in the areas of infant interaction and communication. Within two months, infant girls begin to respond to faces, and they choose to make eye contact with their caregivers. Infant boys, however, are less interested in human interaction. They prefer instead to focus on mobiles suspended above their cribs, and at times they even determinedly squirm away to avoid eye contact. This gender difference in relational responses is maintained throughout life. Women pursue a lifelong quest to establish rapport with others; males concentrate more on discovering how the world around them works.

My (Nancy's) sister Christine recently shared a story concerning her husband, Carl, and it's a good illustration of this point. Carl spent thirty minutes in a phone conversation with his brother. Christine later asked him, "How's everything with Glenn?"

Carl replied, "Fine," which, though not as information intensive as she was hoping to hear, was an accurate one-word summary of Glenn's welfare.

Christine tried to pursue this topic in a little more depth. "How's Mary [Glenn's wife]?"

Answer: "I'm assuming she's fine. He didn't say otherwise."

Since Carl was also watching television, Christine let it go at that. She has learned from experience that even if she tries later to find out more about Glenn and Mary, there will be little information to come. It isn't that Carl is trying to hide anything; it's just that he and his brother talk about their various guy-type interests and not so much about relational stuff.

By contrast, Christine and I will talk for an hour and find out how everyone (including their dog) is doing—but we'll neglect to discuss what Carl considers the biggest news of all, their new TV.

BOTTOM LINE

*If you want your husband to listen to you,
say a little less about Aunt Mary and a
little more about Aunt Mary's new car.*

WIRED, NOT WEIRD

WE'RE SURE YOU KNOW that your husband is far different from you and marriage doesn't cure that. It's the way God made him. On purpose! For a reason!

Being wired differently from you doesn't make your husband weird. It's what makes him a *man*.

To understand him better, here are several facts your husband would like you to know (according to some suggestions we've received in our research). Put these into action, and watch his listening factor soar.

- I am not a mind reader. When something is wrong and I ask you what it is, and you say, "Nothing," I believe you. If you say, "The flowers in the front yard are dying and need water; would you please turn on the sprinkler?" that makes sense to me, and I'll take care of it. If you say, "I wonder why the front yard looks so droopy," that goes right under my radar. My passing thought might be, *Maybe she thinks the ground is shifting. I don't have a clue how to fix that, so I'll just ignore her remark.*

- Stop being so frustrated when I leave the toilet seat up. You can put it down as easily as you expect me to lift it. I'll try to remember, but if I run to the bathroom during a commercial, I may forget to put the seat down. Please just look before you sit.

- If you react angrily to my quirks, I tend to get angry back.

- Sunday afternoon is for viewing sports. It's what I enjoy doing. Allow me my enjoyment. You could learn about it by reading the sports page. It comes every day, and every day it probably contains the results of some game I watched. Better yet, watch sports with me. (Were you just pretending to like them before we got married?)

- Shopping isn't fun for most of us guys. If I suggest we go shopping, it means I need to buy something specific—which I can do in ten minutes or less. Or it could mean I'm trying to please you. If it's the latter, I'm hoping you'll shop really fast—and if you don't mind, I'll wait in the car.

- Please don't cry. Guys don't know what to do with crying women. Tears make us nervous and uncomfortable, and they seem to give you an unfair advantage. In sports terms, crying would be considered a delay of game. Everyone's disappointed, the tarps go down, the people hurry off to their individual dry spots, the vendors get a bit richer...and we just get wet.

- If your birthday's coming and you want something in particular, tell me. I wouldn't guess right even if you hinted for several weeks. And, for heaven's sake, tell me your birthday's coming. Say something like, "Saturday is my birthday, and I'd love it if we could go out for dinner." Don't set me up to disappoint you. If I miss your birthday or blow the gift, it doesn't mean I love you less.

- Yes and no are perfectly acceptable answers to almost every question I ask.

- *Please* don't ask me a loaded question. That's scary to us guys. If you're shaped like an apple, a belt isn't going to look good. And if you don't look good in an outfit while you're standing in front of the mirror, trust the mirror as your friend. Don't make me speak truth you don't want to hear.

- Women's shoes all look alike to us. I'm no help on that subject, so let's not go there. And by the way, if we're shopping together, don't wear shoes that hurt your feet.

- Come to me with a problem only if you want my help solving it. That's what I do. When you have something you just want to talk through, call your mother, your sister, or a girlfriend. I'm a man, and I fix problems. I don't listen endlessly to what he said, what she said, what he wore, what she wore...

- I know your memory is perfect, but I can be forgetful. So let's agree that if we had a disagreement three months ago, I don't remember a thing about it. Let's not dredge up old mud. We will both just end up with dirt on our faces.
- I'm still here, and that means I love you. I don't tell you that a lot, but in all the world, I chose you.

A man doesn't get married with a list of rules in mind to give you. He just expects to live happily ever after. So these "rules" are spoken mostly in self-defense: he wants simply to explain and protect his basic man-ness.

Remember, you married him because he was such a great guy…and he's still the same man. He's a smart guy too. After all, he picked you. He wants to love you…and listen to you…and grow old with you. Help him do just that. Throw your own rulebook away.

BOTTOM LINE

Your husband doesn't want to be married to a whistle-blowing referee.

HIS-AND-HER HORMONES

SINCE YOU WERE A YOUNG GIRL, you've been surging with hormones. They affect everything about you. Every woman is premenstrual, menstrual, postmenstrual, premenopausal, menopausal, or postmenopausal.

Several years ago, after struggling through menopause unaided by medication, I (Nancy) had a problem. I woke up in the middle of the night thinking I was having a heart attack. I couldn't catch my breath, and my heart was racing a mile a minute. My husband called 911, and before long our room was filled with firemen and EMTs. They confirmed I wasn't having a heart attack but told me that I needed to see my doctor in the morning.

I went the next day, and my doctor determined I had a hormone problem. He put me on two prescriptions—and one turned out to be 75 percent more than I needed! But I'm getting ahead of myself. Anyway, as directed, I took the female hormone for twenty days of the month. On the other ten days, I took the high-dosage male hormone (testosterone)—and I turned into a different person. I had no time for bubble baths; I needed a fast shower instead. I had no use for small talk or for anyone doing things in any way other than my own. I corrected even the smallest mistake as though our country were under siege. If my husband loaded the dishwasher, I immediately fixed it, letting him know it was out of the regular order. The other twenty days of the month, I was my normal self.

When I noticed this difference during the second month, I had the prescription changed, and I became my regular self again. All this to say, if testosterone got to me after ten days, can you imagine how it feels to be a man who has testosterone kicking in every second of every day?

It has long been theorized that men think differently than women do. This has been a source of both fascination (during the courtship phase) and endless frustration and confusion (during the marriage stage) of male-female interaction.

Just as testosterone plays an important role in male behavior, estrogen has been shown to impact female brain function and behavior. Specifically, estrogen actually increases the ability of a woman's brain to more rapidly process information between the left and right hemispheres. She talks and acts using both sides of her brain far more than a man does.

A man's brain has more specialized features for each function. Language skills, for instance, are centered mainly in the left hemisphere of a man's brain. A man is therefore far more interested in bare facts than in emotional nuances and extraneous details. His conversational thrust is imparting and processing basic factual information, with far fewer details.

Here's a typical male-female exchange that is often puzzling to both:

Woman (upon her husband's arrival home): "Hi, darling. How was your day?"

Man: "Saw John today. He has a new Pontiac."

At this point, he's looking for responses like these:

(a) "Oh?"

(b) "What year?"

(c) "What engine size?"

(d) "*You* deserve a new car."

But instead he likely gets this response: "A new car? Their old one was so nice. Is he excited about the new car? Is Betty going to drive the old one, or did they trade it in? Did he mention Betty? How are they doing with Tom away at college?"

From the man's perspective, the woman has just brought up exactly the nonessential details he wanted to avoid, half of which have nothing to do with the car. The man is now confused and slightly annoyed that his wife missed the point: John has a new Pontiac. Period. He has no interest whatsoever in listening to her. Meanwhile she's now puzzled that he's suddenly giving one-word answers or mere grunts in response to her further questions.

To avoid this kind of conversation altogether a man may

revert to answering, "Fine," to the question, "How was your day?" This heads you off at the pass. It doesn't mean he doesn't love you. It only means that you two don't approach communication in the same way. When he shared what he did about John and the Pontiac, he was letting you into his world. His world is different. To him, so is yours. It's a brain thing, not a heart thing.

Male-speak is basic and simplified, free of tangential details, and usually meant simply to gather or impart information. It's fact based and unemotional. It usually avoids feelings because that would take him from the concrete informational realm into uncharted territory that may (when his wife is involved) bring a level of discomfort.

Female-speak contains more rich detail and information that men would consider largely irrelevant. To a woman, however, this is the real meat of the story—the emotional context. "What did you say? What did they say? What do you think this means?" Women want to dig deeper into a story. We do this all the time with our girlfriends because we find it fun and interesting. So our husbands' reluctance to share this activity with us seems unfriendly.

BOTTOM LINE

When you and your husband get
off track in conversation, remember that
it's a brain thing, not a heart thing.

9

CONVERSATIONAL GOALS

MEN AND WOMEN HAVE DIFFERENT ways of gathering information. This fact has been documented through brain mapping. This relatively new science tracks brain activity as brain neurons fire in response to various stimuli. In the male brain, between four and six areas process nonverbal signals. Women are far more attuned to unspoken cues. Between fourteen and sixteen areas of the female brain process nonverbal signals—and almost 75 percent of all communication is nonverbal.

Have you ever wondered why your husband seems to miss subtleties in a conversation you are both listening to? Say you're at a party, and you're both chatting with a neighborhood couple. The husband, Gary, is relating a story about their son's soccer game. You notice that Gary's wife, Kate, is standing with her arms folded. She rolls her eyes at one of his comments, contradicts one of his remarks, and doesn't laugh when he makes a small joke.

On the way home you say to your husband, "I wonder what Kate was upset about tonight."

"What do you mean? What makes you think she was upset?"

You can't believe he was so oblivious to the obvious signals Kate was sending. So you let the subject drop.

It isn't that men can't use or understand body language. It's more a matter of focus. In that kind of scenario, your husband is much more likely to be focused on picking up information from Gary's words: the soccer game story. He is possibly not even aware that Kate is also relaying information, which to you is speaking volumes.

Part of a woman's relationship tool kit is the ability to read between the lines. This difference between men and women can be a real stumbling block in husband-wife communication. It's why a woman can have her feelings hurt by a husband who is then completely at a loss as to why she's upset. A man will ask, "What did I say?" The woman responds, "It wasn't what you said. It was the way you said it."

This response leaves him only more puzzled.

Neither men nor women really understand the other's language. As we've said, men are targeting linear content; women are interested in the relational data associated with the content.

This extrasensory ability we women have (with three to four times as many neurons firing in our brains and helping us decipher nonverbal cues) can be either a gift or a curse, especially in marriage. We can choose which it will be—and we do so every day.

Will we be hypersensitive during our husbands' interactions with us? Will we easily take offense at what we consider their lack of sensitivity? Will we become annoyed by their tone or manner and grow cool? Will we be quick to anger and judge or perhaps choose simply to disconnect emotionally?

Or will we use this heightened sensitivity as a blessing, hearing what our husbands are saying through the filter of love rather than criticism? Our family friend Moe uses a lovely phrase when speaking of her husband, Tony: "I know his heart." Put yourself in your husband's shoes. If you were he, would you rather walk on tiptoes, trying not to offend your wife through some unspoken gesture or tone you don't even realize you're using? Or would you rather interact with a woman who trusts that you mean well whatever you do or say?

God has given us women a gift for and interest in building rapport, as well as real skills and sensitivity so that we can do just that. But He offers a warning with these skills: "Use responsibly. For good and not for evil. To build up and not to tear down. For healing and reconciliation. Forgiving offenses as you have been forgiven." In other words, we are to temper this ability with love.

Consider afresh this well-known passage, and make it the filter through which you process every communication:

Love is patient, love is kind. It does not envy, it does not
boast, it is not proud. It is not rude, it is not self-seeking,
it is not easily angered, it keeps no record of wrongs.
Love does not delight in evil but rejoices with the truth.
It always protects, always trusts, always hopes, always
perseveres. Love never fails. (1 Corinthians 13:4–8)

Remember, a man who's loved is most often the one who
considers it a privilege to listen to his wife share her heart.

BOTTOM LINE

Can you say, as Moe does,
"I know his heart"?

10

Rapport Versus Report

Men collect data. Hard, basic data. Bullet-point data. It's the kind of information that goes into a report. Women, however, are more concerned with building rapport and with developing and deepening relationships. We summarize this difference as rapport versus report.

Most women score higher than most men on tests that measure the ability to focus on more than one thing at a time. In a study done by a British institution, men and women were fitted with earphones, each side of which was delivering different information simultaneously. The men were stressed and confused by the test, and they retained almost none of the information. It sounded like jumbled gibberish to them. The women, however, were able to retain the gist of both sets of information, separating the voices and the two sets of content without much difficulty.

This difference in focusing ability helps explain why men don't like to be interrupted while they're watching television. Layers of competing information are difficult for the male brain to process. Either one source of information or the other is likely to be tuned out. And the tuned-out information won't be retained.

So a wife will complain, "But I told you earlier this week we were having friends over tonight!" To which the husband replies, "No, you didn't!" It's no surprise that "earlier this week" was during the Monday-night football game. Since the game was the man's main focus, he didn't retain this secondary information about friends coming over.

Men who are given information they haven't asked for—information that is an "interruption of regularly scheduled programming"—often respond by nodding and saying, "Okay." Doing so eliminates the distraction (the man's goal), but the woman's goal of sharing data isn't achieved. This is not personal. It has to do with focus of brain function in men. And it's hard-wired.

You, as a woman, know how to communicate. Women are born communicators. We know how to tailor our communication to our audience just like today's advertisers do. We communicate differently with our babies than we do with our teenagers, differently with our siblings and family than with our neighbors, differently with our closest friends than with new acquaintances. We know what each person in our lives finds interesting or funny, and we know and make allowances for their shortcomings, as they do for ours. So why don't we tailor our conversation to our husband's unique God-given communication style?

Your gut reaction may well be, "Why should I? Why doesn't he tailor his conversational style to mine?" That is, of course, a fair question. But it isn't going to take you where you want to go—to the land of better communication.

Notice *you* bought this book; he didn't. Sure, he wants to communicate, but he may not be as motivated as you are. Or perhaps he feels he'll fail even if he tries. So, if things are going to improve, you will probably have to take the first steps. And why not? It's an honor to be the one to initiate change in the relationship. Even if he doesn't acknowledge or notice your efforts, God will.

Sometimes we women react to our husbands passive-aggressively—and this isn't a good thing. We want to say, "You never listen!" or, "I'm not as important to you as a ball game!" rather than tailor our conversations to fit them. In other words, we resist doing something for our husbands that we do every day of our lives for our babies, teenagers, friends, and other family members—communicate in ways that fit their unique personalities.

If you really want your husband to hear something, respect his innate, uniquely male quality of singleness of focus by waiting until he isn't involved in other pursuits to talk to him. You can best reach him when he isn't otherwise focused—like when you're driving somewhere together...at the breakfast table...during dinner…on a walk…sitting outside having coffee…or in bed. Be creative.

Also, remember that your husband uses only an average seven thousand words daily compared to your twenty thousand. (Someone recently told us that's because a woman has to say the same thing three times before her husband gets it!) So try to be more concise and less anecdotal in your conversation. Maybe use five thousand of your words for him and save the other fifteen thousand for your women friends, who will find your stories captivating. Don't bury your man under an avalanche of words.

Try to make the experience of conversation with you as pleasant as possible. Men hate conversational openers such as, "We need to talk," "We need to sit down and work on this relationship," or, "How come you never…?" He would rather have a root canal. He loves you, but he's a little afraid he'll somehow push the wrong button if he listens to you very long and responds inappropriately. You're like a sports car that's very snazzy, but tricky to drive.

So be the sports car that's snazzy but simple to drive. This causes your guy to relax…and listen.

BOTTOM LINE

Make listening to you actually be fun.
If he pushes the wrong button,
let it go. The ride will be worth it.

PART 2

How You Shoot Yourself in the Foot

11

Nagging

I (Connie) grew up on a farm, and my grandparents lived just a few miles away. Frequently my sisters and I would ride our bicycles to their house to visit with them.

Grandpa would often talk about the horses he had as a child. "She was just an old nag," he would sometimes say. I knew, even then, that an "old nag" was a tired, worn-out horse that wasn't worth much. Even as a kid, I was struck by the ugliness of the word *nag*.

Being a nag is still ugly—especially to our husbands. It's an even uglier habit—almost always used by a man to describe his wife. Rarely is a husband accused of nagging his wife. In fact, in one reference we checked, the definition included the phrase "especially women." Another source described nagging as "feminine in nature."

If your husband's perception of you is that you nag him on a fairly regular basis, he'll care less about listening to you. It doesn't matter whether or not you see yourself as a nag. If your husband considers you a nag, he'll tune you out. Why? Men loathe nagging, and they will go to any length to avoid it—which includes tuning out the deliverer of the unwanted words.

Nagging is universally regarded as a negative behavior, yet it remains a problem for couples today. In fact, it ranked near the top when men listed major problem areas in their marriages.

Once a man labels his wife a nag (even though he might not outwardly say so), from that point on, he'll tend to respond to her as a nag regardless of whether she's nagging and even when her intentions are pure and sincere. After all, for every negative statement you make toward someone (and nagging is definitely negative), it takes from ten to twenty positive statements to reverse it. Once you're considered a nag by your husband, it will take much effort on your part for him to see you otherwise.

At its root, nagging is really about two things:

1. *Control.* A woman often believes, *If I harp long enough, I can get you to do what I want you to do.* But the reality is, you can't. You can't control another person's choice.

2. *Pride.* While a woman may not verbalize this, she's most likely thinking, *My way is best. It makes the most sense. In fact, my way is how 99 percent of America would do it. I'm not bugging my husband because I want my way. I'm bugging him because my way is better. Why can't he see that?*

We probably can all offer a short (or long) list of things we wish our husbands would or wouldn't do. Things involving toothpaste caps, clothes on the floor, toilet seats, messes on countertops, broken things, remote control hogging... Whatever it is you resent, if you nag him about it, before long you'll begin to deeply resent the person behind the habit as well. The same man you once considered your darling.

So how do we deal with these irritants? Because you can be sure that if your attempts to reform his behavior escalate into nagging, his resolve to ignore you will increase. Let's say, for example, that you point out to him a particular problem and the fact that it annoys you. Which of these will be his response?

- Distressed that this behavior has displeased you, your husband reforms and never repeats it again. (We're pretty sure that unless your husband is a rare exception, this one won't apply.)
- He continues the offending behavior as if you've never said a word about it.
- For the sake of peace and quiet, he eventually changes and does it your way, but he harbors resentment.

The final option may look to you like a win for you, but it's a huge relationship loss. You see, nagging brings about a seething resentment in your husband that causes him to withdraw and feel angry toward you. He usually won't voice this anger, but he's feeling it nonetheless. He loathes your attempts to change him, and he resents being treated like a child.

Let's recap. Nagging arises from resentment in a wife because her husband won't change. And nagging brings about resentment in her husband because he feels she's trying to control him by treating him like a five-year-old. (Don't forget that your husband wants to be your knight...your warrior...your slayer of dragons.) It's not hard to see that nagging is a lose-lose situation. It helps no one.

So what's a woman to do? The following scenario may offer a solution.

Let's say some kind of maintenance needs to be done around the house or in the yard, your husband knows it, and you're annoyed that he hasn't done it. After reminding him once or twice about the task, you have two choices. First, you can leave it for him to deal with on his own time. Each of our husbands used to say to us—as we were nagging them—that when the issue bothered them enough, they would take care of it. But we never let things reach that point before we began our tirades.

Now for your second choice: you yourself can do whatever needs doing. We've learned from experience that it's often easier to just do whatever it is that's bothering you. It has rarely taken excessive time, and we have often found ourselves wondering what the big deal was to start with. We try to do the task with an "as unto You, Lord" attitude. We say in our hearts—and sometimes out loud—"God, thank You for my home, my husband, my children. Thank You that I'm physically able to do so many things. And right now I'm doing this task with You in mind, hoping my attitude and my actions are pleasing to You."

Somehow, in some mysterious way, you're suddenly doing more than just a menial task. You're offering up a sacrificial gift to God. You're putting others before yourself. You're engaged in the practice of humility, which is a behavior God esteems.

Now here's the hard part. Whichever of the two choices you make: after making your choice, *let it go*. Don't continue nagging or tell him that you've done "his" job.

Not long ago, I (Nancy) spoke to Ray about a window box that had fallen off our house during a rainstorm. It had been on the front of the house, fully planted and beautifully blooming. I left the box where it fell, tidying it up a bit. Then I mentioned it to Ray and let it go. That's the choice I most often make now, but for many years of my marriage I didn't.

Besides being healthy for a marriage, your refusal to nag your husband can bode well for you in other areas, too—and when you least expect it. For example, a few years ago Connie and I were invited to be guests on the radio program *Family Life Today* with Dennis Rainey. We had taped about twelve consecutive thirty-minute segments with them. After that much recording work, I was—as Connie puts it—"tard." But we still had more to do, and Dennis suggested that for the thirteenth segment we talk about nagging.

Because I was so weary, I just blurted out, "Dennis, I never nag Ray."

"Get Ray on the phone," Dennis suddenly insisted. "We're going to check this out on national radio." I was so discombobulated that I couldn't even think of Ray's phone number. Connie was laughing hysterically at me, and so was Dennis. I was a nervous wreck. Ray is a man of integrity, and he's also quite blunt. What if he completely disagreed with this statement I never should have made in the first place?

I finally came up with the number, and we got Ray on the phone. By that point my head was on the table, and I was a rubbery mess. I heard Dennis say, "Ray, we've got Connie and Nancy in the studio, and Nancy is telling us she never nags you. Is that true?"

Time was suspended for a moment. Then I heard my husband say, "You know, she never does."

At that moment, those were the sweetest words I'd ever heard. I was so thankful—and still horrified that I'd even brought up the subject in the first place.

Our window box still needs to be reinstalled. I'm sure Ray will notice it, and at some point he will probably fix it. But that's not a task I've ever done. If it sits on the ground, the world won't come to an end for me. It's not a big deal.

I know I wasn't always like this. But I also know I never want to be a nag again.

It is better to dwell in a corner of the housetop [on the flat oriental roof, exposed to all kinds of weather] than in a house shared with a nagging, quarrelsome, and fault-finding woman. (Proverbs 21:9, AMP)

BOTTOM LINE

Nagging is a lose-lose proposition.

NONVERBAL COMMUNICATION AND LOVE LANGUAGES

HOW WELL DO YOU KNOW WHAT your husband *believes* he's saying? So much of love is unspoken. Anyone who's ever loved a dog or cat knows how true this is, how much love can be communicated nonverbally.

Chances are your husband isn't comfortable expressing his love in the poetic language you would find in a greeting card. But he thinks he's demonstrating his love for you in many other ways. He assumes, for instance, that when he washes your car and fills it with gas, you see this as love.

We'll never forget overhearing this brief but devastating illustration of poor communication:

Wife: "You never tell me you love me."

Husband: "I don't have to tell you. I married you, didn't I?"

If you share this exchange with men and women, you get different reactions. Women are horrified that a husband would make such a cold and seemingly unfeeling response to his wife's plea for words of affirmation. Men, however, think this is a reasonable response. Men understand that this man is showing his love to his wife by his continued commitment to her in marriage. In other words, talk is cheap, and actions speak louder than words.

Does your husband even know what to do or say that would make you feel loved? Not knowing each other's love language creates a huge opportunity for misunderstanding. It can add enormous stress to a marriage relationship. It can even lead to divorce.

Gary Chapman has given us excellent tools for avoiding this pitfall in his wonderful book *The Five Love Languages.* He helps us see that whatever makes your husband feel most loved is usually the method he'll choose when attempting to demonstrate his own love for you.

With that in mind, read over the following descriptions of different ways to express your love for your husband. You might try ranking them in order of their importance to him:

My husband feels most loved when I...

- *use physical touch, such as giving him a back rub or massaging his feet.* (Love Language: Physical Contact)
- *get his morning coffee and paper, run his errands, and so on.* (Love Language: Acts of Service)

- *praise his good attributes and express encouraging words.* (Love Language: Words of Affirmation)
- *surprise him by buying him a present.* (Love Language: Gifts)
- *watch his favorite TV show with him, or do something else together.* (Love Language: Quality Time)

Whatever ranked highest gives you an insight into what love looks like to your husband, and this is most often how he'll express it back to you. He may be giving you gifts when you long to simply spend time together. If Gifts isn't his love language, he might not appreciate your gifts as much as you'd like, and he might even ask you not to continue spending money on those kinds of things. When you can identify your husband's love language(s), you're more likely to see how he's operating in that language to demonstrate his love for you.

My (Nancy's) brother-in-law's love language is Acts of Service, so on his birthday my sister, Christine, cooks his favorite dinner and gives him a manicure and a facial. Before she understood this, she would buy him a gift each year. He would almost always look frustrated even before he opened it, then say, "Can this be returned?" It would leave her hurt and completely confused, because she loves getting presents. She wondered why he wouldn't just say, "Thank you so much! It's wonderful."

After years of misunderstanding, Christine now knows he practices frugality in order to save for their retirement. Gifts—giving as well as receiving them—just isn't his love language.

Now that she's aware of this, she's come to notice his many unheralded acts of service. In all the years of their marriage—twenty-nine—she has never once had to ask him to take out the trash. He also sees to it that her car is always clean and she always has gasoline in the tank. He's an Acts of Service man, and she has learned to appreciate this greatly.

One more word about this language of love. Many men see their careers as their Act of Service—working hard to advance in their chosen professions in order to provide for their families. A wife tends to see this hard work as neglect of her and their quality time together.

It's vitally important that we understand each other's love language. We've all seen men devastated by what was, to them, an unexpected divorce. They're unable to understand how this could have happened when, as the husband says, "I gave her everything I thought would make her happy."

So make it a quest, like a search for hidden treasure, to decode your husband's various love languages and put them into action. Likewise, each time you recognize he's using his love language, tell yourself, "He loves me." And don't neglect to express your delight to him.

BOTTOM LINE

Are you hearing what your
husband's actions are saying?

Jumping to Conclusions

Have you ever tried to read your husband's mind to determine his mood? It's usually not a good idea, because we never know what another person—especially a man—is thinking.

Here's an example:

Wife's Diary

Tonight I thought he was acting weird. We'd made plans to meet at a restaurant to have dinner. I thought he was upset that I was a bit late, but he made no comment. Conversation wasn't flowing, so I suggested we go somewhere private so we could talk. He agreed, but he kept quiet.

I asked him what was wrong, but he said, "Nothing."

I asked him if it was my fault that he was upset. He said it had nothing to do with me and not to worry.

On the way home I told him I loved him. He simply smiled and kept driving. I can't explain his behavior; I don't know why he didn't say, "I love you too."

When we got home, I felt as if I'd lost him, as if he wanted nothing to do with me anymore. He just sat there and watched TV. He seemed distant and absent. Finally I decided to go to bed. About ten minutes later he came to bed. To my surprise he responded to my caress, and we made love. But I still felt he was distracted and his thoughts were somewhere else.

After he fell asleep, I cried. I don't know what to do. I'm almost sure his thoughts are with someone else. My life is a disaster.

Husband's Diary

I didn't catch any fish today, but at least I made love with my beautiful wife.

If a woman is quiet, she's often upset or hurt. So she assumes the same when her husband is quiet. But most of the time a man's quietness has nothing to do with his wife.

A woman will often become emotional in her efforts to draw out her husband. This causes him to become frustrated and withdraw. To counter this, the female continues talking to reengage him, which is even more frustrating to the man. At this point, he'll often disengage from the conversation altogether.

Women conclude from this kind of interaction that something is wrong in the relationship, and they try to hash things out. The poor husband doesn't know what to say. He simply wants to be himself, but often this isn't acceptable to his wife.

A man's silence is normal, especially when he feels he's being interrogated. He simply stops listening and thinks of something more pleasant—like getting some peace and quiet or catching more fish next time.

BOTTOM LINE

*Men relish silence, and it usually
has nothing to do with their
feelings toward their wives.*

THE HA-HA'S

MY HUSBAND AND I (NANCY) LOVE to go to London. It's so different from any place we've ever been. We've toured much of the city but never ventured out to the English countryside, to places my friend Diane has told me about. She spoke of the great English manors with their exquisitely designed gardens, perfectly pruned hedges, and flowers of every kind. She said that you can even see deer grazing in the distance…

Connie and I have visited our publisher's office in a small town in Oregon. We couldn't help but notice the town's beauty, and also the great numbers of wandering deer. They seem to enjoy eating anything planted low to the ground. So homes are surrounded by munched-on hedges, spotty flower gardens, and small trees with leaves missing on the lower branches…

Diane explained the difference between the English manors and the Oregon homes. She said an English manor will be surrounded by a wide, deep trench, hidden by bushes, that keeps the deer at bay. These grazers can't get to the manor's gardens because of this *ha-ha,* the name given to such a trench.

What is keeping your husband away from you? Have you built a trench so wide he doesn't even try to cross over? Is it possible that he feels he's become a mere fixture in your home or is taking second place to your children? Does he no longer feel invited into your manor?

This dynamic often results when a husband travels. While he's gone for days at a time, you run the estate, firmly entrenched in controlling the daily and nightly routine. Upon his return, he seems like a bothersome guest. This attitude is contagious and can affect your children. When your husband feels he's no longer welcome in his own home, he loses something he so desperately needs in life—to be valued and respected by his family. Who would want to cozy up to a woman and listen lovingly to her when there's a No Trespassing sign like this hanging over her head?

If this description provides a glimpse into your own interaction with your husband, there are several things you can do:

- Pray that God will give you the grace to be loving and respectful.
- Take a few moments before he gets home to pick up the house.
- Have his favorite dinner waiting.
- Greet him warmly at the door with a hug and a ten-second kiss.

- Smile.
- Before you start telling him everything that has happened to you and the kids while he's been gone, turn all your attention to him, his words, and his needs.
- Get him a glass of ice water.
- Stroke his back and neck.
- Whisper sexual innuendos in his ear.
- Make bedtime romantic.

Do you think a man treated like that will want to listen?

BOTTOM LINE

Ha-ha's will keep away deer, but your warmest welcome will entice your dear.

15

WOMEN WAY OVERTHINK

I (NANCY) RECENTLY HEARD A STORY of a husband and wife in bed, each on far opposite sides. The middle of the bed was empty, but the woman's thoughts were not: *I wonder if he still loves me. All he does is stare at the ceiling. I'll bet he's noticed I've gained weight. He never talks to me, and it's driving me crazy. I don't know what to do. I feel so lonely.*

The husband was in fact looking at the ceiling. He thought, *How can a spider crawl upside-down on its feet and not fall?*

It was as simple as that. This is classic overthinking.

One evening not long ago, Ray came home from work acting grouchy. I wondered what I'd done. I didn't agonize to the extent that the woman in the cartoon did, but I definitely wondered if his sour mood had something to do with me. In case it did, I developed a great plan to cheer him up the next day (which was my day off from work). The next morning Ray told me he'd been rehashing in his mind a conversation with a friend that hadn't gone well. Ray's grouchiness wasn't about me after all, but I stuck with my cheer-him-up plan anyway.

When he came home for lunch (he works only two miles away), he walked in the door and found a TV tray set up and holding a roast beef sandwich with tomatoes, chips, a Hostess Twinkie, four small crackers with little slices of cheese on them, a glass of ice water, and a small bottle of chocolate milk. He was ecstatic. (Ray's a huge food guy.)

For dinner that evening, it was filet mignon steaks and baked potatoes. Ray sliced some melon for us, and we ended the meal with caramel sundaes. He was raving about the meal with every bite. When we got up the next morning, he was still raving about it. Ray was his happy self once again.

Through the years I've learned what makes Ray happy. And making him happy actually causes him to listen to me more attentively than ever. I'll admit that sometimes when he's feeling down, I'll still think it's my fault and I'll go over and over in my mind what I could have done. But I've learned this lesson: when a man who usually interacts with his wife is quiet all of a sudden, it's not usually about his wife. So don't overthink!

BOTTOM LINE

Trying to read between the lines
will drive you nuts.

16

Don't Ask If You Don't Want an Answer

WHEN A MAN ASKS A QUESTION, he wants a direct answer. If he says to his wife, "Does this shirt look good with these pants?" he wants either a yes or a no. Either answer is acceptable, and neither will hurt his feelings. Most important, neither answer reflects in any way his wife's love for him.

A man assumes all this is true when his wife asks him a question. "Does this outfit look good on me?" says to him:

- Either yes or no will be an acceptable answer.
- Neither will hurt your feelings.
- Neither reflects in any way his love for you.

Yet we women can get our feelings hurt, can't we? And

although a man is always trying to solve his wife's problems, hurt feelings are one thing he simply doesn't know how to fix.

Suppose a woman says, "Sue hurt my feelings at work today, and I don't know what to do. How do you think I should handle it?"

This is a nightmare problem for a man. *Feelings.* Might as well ask him to go to ballet class with you. He'd really rather have you bring him something he can fix with duct tape, WD-40, or a screwdriver. He likes going into his manly hard-drive brain to come up with solutions, but when a feelings problem needs a fix, he often reacts in a defensive mode. He may even sound angry, even though he's not: "Well, what in the world do you expect me to do about that?" At this point, in the wife's mind, not only has Sue jumped down her throat, but her husband has as well.

What a woman wants at such a time is for her man to say, "How dare anyone hurt your feelings! You, who are always kind to everyone! Sue must have been having a really bad day." And if he follows these words with a tender hug, he will have slain the dragon. But guys don't typically understand this—and we hold it against them when they don't. That's foolishness on our part.

A marriage can go on like this for years. She asks a question, and he answers it. Her feelings get hurt, and he can't understand why. Now she's even more hurt because he can't understand that he hurt her feelings. He also feels like he can never say the right thing, no matter how hard he tries.

This is a crazy way to live, and we suggest you be the one to stop this crazy cycle. How? It's simple: don't ask your husband any question you don't want answered. If you prefer to process something with him and merely have him listen to your processing, then tell him this up front. Otherwise, he'll try to come up with an answer while you're speaking, and he'll interrupt you the second he does. Let him know at the outset that his only responsibility is to listen. That is something he can do, but he needs to know that to do it.

By the way, your husband won't want to do this only-listening thing very often because it makes no sense to him. He's an action man. A problem solver. A warrior. A knight in shining armor. In his mind, he truly is all these things, and he should be so in your mind too.

It's not in a man's nature to sit passively by and merely listen for hours on end without doing something about the situation being described. If what you're really seeking is reassurance and love, tell him! Don't ask a veiled question that sets him up for disaster when you're actually fishing for reassurance. The pond you're fishing in isn't stocked with that kind of fish.

We need to learn to be more direct and to the point. Learning to ask for what we need is a huge step for us women—and a huge relief for the men in our lives. So, if you need reassurance and love, tell him you're feeling vulnerable and need a little reassurance and love. This isn't hard, and it doesn't mean you're not a strong woman. In fact, asking for what you need takes great strength.

For example: "Honey, I feel so vulnerable right now. I'm not sure what's going on. [Or if you are sure, let him know!] This feeling just hit me from out of the blue. I don't understand it, so I sure don't expect you to. [He'll be instantly relieved.] But what would help me so much right now is if you would just hold me tight. You don't have to say anything. [He'll be even more relieved.] I just need to feel your arms around me."

Your husband can do that. He can do what you're asking him. He probably doesn't understand how that's really going to help anything, but he loves you and he'll do it for you. He'll probably even be amazed to find that doing so makes him feel like more of a warrior than ever. He's protecting his damsel in a way that's unusual to him. He might even mention this to his buddies at work. The heroine has been rescued—largely because the heroine set him up with a clearly stated and very doable request. This is a win-win situation for the two of you.

Of course, your husband will completely forget that he was told exactly what to do, and if you're wise, you won't remind him of that—ever. He'll begin seeing himself in a whole new light, and he'll like what he sees. It makes him feel like a man, not a failure, which is how too many married men feel today. And all it took was a straightforward, honest, to-the-point request from you.

In sharp contrast to the preceding scenario, suppose you'd

hinted and sighed and been sad and weepy, yet never told your husband exactly what he could do to make you feel better. He would have made some sort of masculine attempt to make you feel better, or maybe he would have done nothing at all. He might even have left the house and gone to see a movie until you got over whatever it was that was bothering you. (Two if not three of these responses would have made you even more hurt or angry.)

When you act like that, your husband is like a man stumbling around in a dark room. But when you tell him exactly how to comfort you, it's as if you turn on the light for him.

This is a huge principle to grasp. Don't think that because he's a grown man he should know where the light switch is. He doesn't. He knows where it is for *him,* but not where it is for you. He may be searching in a completely different room—or even a different house.

So help him out! Your Direct Talk helps your husband help you—and that helps everybody! Direct Talk also serves as a healthy model for your children. It's good for them to observe straightforward interactions between you and their dad. Frustrated moms don't make the kinds of memories they want their kids to have.

When it comes to having your husband help meet your emotional needs, the more specific you can be, the better. Most men get nervous when their wives express outright that they're in need of some sort of emotional shoring up. Women know exactly what that desired reassurance and love look like, but men do not. So this is definitely land-mine territory to a man. He doesn't want to say or do the wrong thing, but he knows he's supposed to say or do something. So draw him a picture and, even then, give lots of grace. When it comes to these emotional issues, you can't be too specific…or too forgiving.

Whenever your man attempts to comfort you emotionally, recognize and appreciate his efforts, no matter what. Your feedback encourages and motivates him more than you know, and he'll be more apt to be up for the challenge the next time. The last thing you want to do is criticize your husband when he's trying his best to meet an emotional need you've expressed. He'll soon stop trying even if you're using Direct Talk. You can talk directly until you're blue in the face, but if you criticize his efforts when he's trying to do what you ask, he'll quickly realize that facing a firing squad has better odds. He simply won't keep putting himself in the position to have you shoot him down.

Remember, in almost every interaction with your husband, you can't go wrong if you continue to remind yourself: *Build him up. Don't tear him down.* Men seem to love it when their wives even exaggerate a bit in this area:

- "Oh, that makes me feel soooooooo much better!"
- "You give the best hugs of anyone I know."
- "I can't tell you how much at ease I feel."
- "You make me feel so safe." (Men *love* making their wives feel safe.)

We've worked with a number of women who often tell us they simply don't talk like this. Our answer: "It's time you did."

For heaven's sake, the man is your husband! And few things please your husband more than knowing he's a winner in making his wife feel loved and secure. And few things warm him up to listening to you like these kinds of remarks do.

A quick afterthought: Have you ever asked your husband if he feels loved and secure as a husband…if he feels respected? Or does he seem so emotionally disconnected that you just assume he has no emotional needs?

Your husband does have emotional needs, but few men feel comfortable talking about them, especially to a wife who is never emotionally content herself (he'll put your needs first) or who is generally critical. Critical wives aren't safe to share much of anything with, let alone one's emotions. And critical wives aren't the kind of women husbands want to listen to either.

Finally, does your husband know beyond a shadow of a doubt that you love him…admire him…and would take a bullet for him? Could he list three things you find noteworthy in him? Have you told him lately he's a wonderful lover? Have you recently expressed appreciation for how he provides for his family? Reassuring statements like these are huge to a guy, but we tend to forget making them, because we're too often more focused on our own emotional needs.

But that's what losers do—focus on themselves. You're not a

loser. You're a child of God. And one of the holiest things you can ever do on this earth is to respect your husband and make sure he knows he's of great worth to you.

BOTTOM LINE

*Tell your husband today
how priceless he is to you.*

Who Influences You?

SOMETIMES, WITHOUT EVEN REALIZING IT, a woman does a foolish thing. She allows the actions or words of another person to control how she behaves. A woman is usually unaware when she does this, and later, she may feel unable to reclaim her power. Let us offer an example.

When Kim married Steve, she knew his mother had a strong personality and was the one who ruled the family. Everyone went out of the way to make sure Steve's mother was happy—because if Mama wasn't happy, no one was happy. In fact, if Mama wasn't happy, it was torturous for everyone else. The unspoken rule of the family was simple: "Keep Mama happy at all costs." Kim sometimes thought she should needlepoint this phrase and nail it to every door in the house.

If Steve's mom fell into a bad mood or became tired and irritable, people walked on eggshells to make certain they didn't irritate her further. What had caused her sudden mood change never mattered, not that she would tell them. Regardless of the cause, everyone immediately jumped into the "we must please Mama" mode and racked their brains to try to get her back into a good mood. Often, family members would just end up going to a movie so she could be alone, and they hoped things would be better when they returned. Usually, though, the change in mood took at least a day or two; sometimes her prickly behavior even stretched out for weeks.

The fact that everyone lived in such fear of her mother-in-law struck Kim as odd. These people, now in their forties and fifties, were constantly jumping through hoops for this woman. Kim occasionally remarked to Steve about the tremendous amount of energy everyone expended to keep Mama in a good mood. He would just shrug his shoulders and sigh.

Now, Kim was gracious by nature, and she generally managed to avoid any major disagreements with her mother-in-law. There had been occasional remarks, but nothing too severe. Then, one July day, Steve and Kim dropped by his parents' house just to say hello.

Mama wasn't in a good mood, and at one point, as they sat around the kitchen table and drank iced tea, she made a cutting remark directed at Kim. She followed it with another. Then another. Kim was speechless. She waited for Steve to stand up for her, but he didn't. Steve acted on his instincts, which was to go straight into survival mode: say nothing and hope the storm will quickly pass.

Kim then looked toward her father-in-law. Surely he would say something. No such luck. He was in the same mode as Steve. Kim quickly surmised she was on her own. What she did next amazes her still to this day: she slipped into survival mode as well. She sat quietly and endured her mother-in-law's disparaging remarks. Somehow over the years, without even realizing it, she'd apparently bought into the number one rule herself. Keep Mama happy—even if it costs your self-respect.

Later, she and Steve said their awkward good-byes and left. Kim was fuming by the time they reached the car. Steve had never seen her so upset. Sure, Kim was upset with his mother, but she was outraged at Steve's inability to stand up for her. Kim was absolutely furious, and she told him as much in no uncertain terms.

He tried to defend himself, and he even suggested that what his mother said "wasn't all that bad." This comment enraged Kim even more, and they fought all the way home. No matter what Steve said, Kim trumped his remark with one of her own. Steve felt bad for not coming to his wife's defense, and he was humiliated by his lack of courage and failure to stand up to his mother. He heaved a big sigh and let Kim vent. He'd slipped into survival mode again—for the second time that evening. He knew from experience what to do: apologize profusely, lie low the rest of the night, and pray the storm would quickly pass.

But it didn't. Kim was still angry the next morning…and the next morning…and the next morning. And for many more mornings after that. Other than cursory remarks, she barely spoke to Steve. She wasn't going to let this one go easily. If she did, she was afraid Steve wouldn't learn his lesson.

(May we just interject at this point that it's not a wife's responsibility to make sure her husband "learns his lesson." Say what's on your mind, let it go, and then trust God to use whomever or whatever He chooses to work in your husband's life. May we further interject that Kim was, without even noticing it, hovering close to the dangerous precipice of becoming exactly like her mother-in-law: *Kim wasn't happy, so nobody was happy.*)

At first Steve attempted to get things back to normal. After so long, though, he didn't know what to do. Sure, his mother shouldn't have said what she did, and he shouldn't have let her. But it wasn't akin to murder.

Unfortunately, though, as Kim said later, it was akin to murder in her mind—the murder of her spirit. And she wasn't about to let the incident go until Steve apologized "enough." Steve thought he'd already apologized way more than enough. He had no idea that his "enough" barely registered in Kim's mind. At some point, he began shutting down just as Kim had. He would fight fire with fire—or, in this case, coldness with coldness. He was tired of being treated with such utter disrespect.

Kim and Steve almost lost their marriage over this issue.

Certainly other issues led up to that fateful day, but the attack on Kim by Steve's mother was the almost-fatal stroke. And compounding that was a development at Steve's work. Steve had always been devoted to his family, but he found himself suddenly drawn to a woman in his office. She was consistently warm and friendly, and she complimented him frequently. Plus, she treated him with such respect—which he sure wasn't getting on the home front. One day he realized he was headed down a slippery slope: the gal in the office held far more interest to him than the gal at home.

Now, Steve and Kim had gone through tough times before, but one had always been there to rally the other through. This time, though, neither cared enough to rally.

Kim was still mad, but she was finally starting to speak to Steve in two-word sentences instead of just one. The woman in his office, however, spoke in full, flowing paragraphs, with almost every word laced with admiration.

By the grace of God, Steve decided to pick up the phone, call his pastor, and get help. To his surprise, the pastor was neither shocked nor surprised. He assured Steve that together they would work through this thing.

For the first time in a long while, Steve felt hope. He talked to Kim, and she agreed to speak with the pastor as well. He helped her work through her anger and resentment toward not only Steve but his mother as well. He also taught her how to confront people appropriately when they acted inappropriately.

Slowly, Steve and Kim got back on track. Steve's heart was back with his family. He set firm boundaries with the woman in his office, and she and her husband were soon transferred out of state—the kind of physical distance that experts say is of utmost importance if an inappropriate attachment between two people occurs.

Maybe you're surprised that the woman in the office was married, because you can't imagine a married woman getting as emotionally involved with Steve as she did. Yes, they do…and so could you. If you think this is something that couldn't happen to you, you leave this part of your life unprayed for and leave yourself open to attack. We often think we fail in our weak areas, but often our areas of strength—such as believing we are immune to adultery and emotional affairs—can bring us down. This woman's marriage was just as lonely for her as Steve's was for him. Two lonely marriages make great kindling for a roaring fire! These are the same words God used in regard to man being alone: *It is not good* (see Genesis 2:18). Never forget that.

Today Kim and Steve would say that the "day Mom roared at Kim" was a turning point in their marriage. What man meant for evil, God used for good. Steve began standing up to his mother, which eventually caused much of her manipulative behavior to cease. Kim learned how to stand up for herself and how to let go of things rather than carry a grudge for days and weeks on end.

Kim learned an even bigger lesson as well. What she'd done,

she realized, was give her power to her mother-in-law. She had temporarily given away control of her life—and almost control of her marriage—to someone else. She had allowed her marriage to teeter on the brink of destruction—all because of the remarks of a harsh, unhappy woman.

Never allow another person to impact your behavior for the worse. Ask God to give you the strength to be a woman of dignity and grace, even during difficult times.

Kim had every right to express her feelings to her mom-in-law and then leave the house. She had every right to express how she felt to Steve. She had every right to speak with someone about the situation and encourage her husband to do so as well. Then, after doing what she could to rectify this problem, she needed to *let it go* and stop holding a grudge against Steve. A man's heart can grow cold living with a cold woman, day after day. The flip side is true as well: a man's heart can grow warm living with a warm woman, day after day.

Permitting another person to influence your behavior can wreak destruction in your own life as well as in the lives of those you love the most. It's devastating to your relationship with the Lord, who commands us to forgive others their trespasses (see Mark 11:25–26). There's never any true power apart from Him.

If Steve hadn't sought help from his pastor, he could well be juggling a schedule now that included a wife, an ex-wife, children from his first marriage, stepchildren, difficult holidays, visitation rights, and the ongoing guilt of having walked out on his family.

Such a chain of events would be traced back to one woman with chronic inappropriate behavior (Steve's mother) and a second woman (Kim) who allowed external influences to determine her choices.

Don't be baited into becoming less than God created you to be. He made you to be *you*. He created you in His image.

What does this truth have to do with your husband listening to you? Just about everything.

BOTTOM LINE

You were created by God to be gracious,
loving, forgiving, and kind. Be you!

PART 3

OPENING HIS HEART OPENS HIS EARS

A Thankful Heart

SEVERAL YEARS AGO ELISABETH ELLIOT came to our church and spoke before a gathering of about two thousand women. We'd seldom seen our church so packed. The event included a question-and-answer session in which she responded to previously submitted questions.

The first note she read and responded to was from a woman who said she had a wonderful husband, four great children, and a nice home. Plus, she loved the Lord. But she felt something was missing. She confided that she just wasn't happy.

Elisabeth has a way of saying what she means, and her reply to this woman's question was unforgettable. She responded, "Your trouble, my dear, is that you don't have a thankful heart."

Do you?

Any one of us can lack a thankful heart. It happens when we

stop counting our blessings and begin listing our woes and griev-
ances instead. It happens to women every day of the week.

If you've lost your delight in being a wife, isn't it time to
count the blessings God has given you rather than being self-
absorbed about your happiness?

Joy—a fruit of the Spirit, activated through a Christ-centered
life—can be the hallmark of your life every day, no matter what
your circumstances (see Galatians 5:22). You'll know joy if you
immerse yourself in the One who created the concept of home
and the relationship of marriage.

We've asked this question before, but we want to ask it
again: Is your husband lonely? Is home the loneliest place he
knows? If so, God says, "That's not good."

After Adam was created, God said this about him: "It is not
good (sufficient, satisfactory) that the man should be alone; I
will make him a helper meet (suitable, adapted, complementary)
for him" (Genesis 2:18, AMP). God is saying "not good" about an
aspect of His very own creation, something He Himself made!
Isn't that unfathomable?

And what—or who—could be brought in to make it good?
Woman! Eve was missing from the life of Adam.

Are you missing—emotionally or otherwise—from the life
of your husband? Some women who would never divorce their
husbands physically think nothing of divorcing them emotionally and sexually. If you're missing from your marriage in these

important ways, won't you resolve to do something about it? Your husband will never want to listen to or have meaningful interaction with a woman who's present in body only, but whose heart and soul are no longer with him.

There's something so refreshing about a woman whose heart is full of thanksgiving. It's as if she sings a different song than the rest of us do. For too long, both of us sang the wrong song: the song of waiting on our husbands to change before we treated them in a kind, respectful manner. No wonder our husbands didn't care to listen to us. We were the living reflections of desolate, thankless hearts.

As we write that, we're reminded of a friend who spent months admiring her neighbor's husband. He was outgoing, handy around the house, and seemed so comfortable with himself, plus he kept himself in excellent physical condition—traits very different from our friend's husband. She often found herself wishing her husband would be more like Mr. Neighbor.

Then one day Mrs. Neighbor came over and shared that her husband had left her and the kids for another woman.

This put a completely different spin on how our friend saw her own husband. Maybe he had two left hands, but he was devoted to her and the children. Sure, he was a bit shy socially, but he never flirted with other women, and in fact, he went out of his way to guard himself against moral failure. And the extra twenty pounds he carried? How many times had he told her how much he loved her cooking? More than she could count. And how long had it been since she'd complimented him for anything? Longer than she could remember.

She began that day to be thankful for her husband. She was surprised how quickly her thankless heart became full again. How she viewed her husband made all the difference in the world. She'd put on a new pair of "glasses." She calls them her Thanksgiving Glasses.

The world can be cruel, and it has probably been far harder on your husband than he lets you know. Men don't typically share these burdens, even with their wives. They want to protect their wives against such worries. Men also want to be found worthy of their wives' respect, so they are reluctant to expose anything that might be perceived as weakness or that might be criticized.

A word to the wise: Should your husband entrust you with something important to him, receive it as such. Don't belittle it, critique it, or betray his trust. He may tell you, "I lost my train of thought at a meeting today, and it was scary."

Reassure him. Be his safe place. Be thankful he chose to share with you something he'll probably not share with another soul.

And don't break your husband's trust. Don't announce the incident at Thanksgiving dinner. Or use it against him the next time *you* forget something ("Well, I can forget too, can't I? Of course, *you* forgot your point in front of a whole room full of people!"). If you treat his cares with loving sensitivity, he'll learn that he can trust you with all the things that are important to him, and he'll share those with you.

Your husband wants to be able to tell you this stuff. And he wants to hear what a woman of wisdom has to say about such things. He's just not sure whether you'll make him regret his confidence in you.

Don't ever make him regret it. If you do, he may not mention his regret. But it steals something away from him that was never meant to be taken, especially by his wife.

If you're guilty of betraying your husband's confidences in the past, you can begin to give back to him what you took away. How? By being thankful.

It's as simple as that. A man married to a thankful woman is often the first man to care about what she's saying.

BOTTOM LINE

Thankfulness should be a way of life.

LET GO OF
ONE THING

WHEN MY (CONNIE'S) TWIN DAUGHTERS were second-graders, they were very excited about being big enough to learn "real" math. So in the evenings Wes and I practiced with them. They progressed well, but there was one pairing they could never remember: three plus four equals seven.

We went over and over that equation with them, but almost every single time, they blanked on it. One of them finally said, "Oh, I just wish they'd take that out, and we'd never have to remember it again."

Another night I remember being in the next room when I heard the girls ask, "Daddy, will you go over our math with us?" Wes was more than happy to, and I heard him begin the drills. The girls took turns answering, and I could tell by their voices they were having fun. Pretty much old pros at this by now, they were blitzing through the tables pretty quickly.

And then I heard Wes call out the dreaded pairing: "Three plus four."

I don't know whose turn it was to answer, but no answer came forth. Wes turned to the other daughter and asked her. Still no answer. Just a lot of thinking and a lot of silence. I stopped what I was doing and listened. Mental telepathy obviously doesn't run in our family because every fiber of my being was willing the girls to say, "Seven."

After what seemed like an eternity of silence, one of them called out, "Eight." (Or maybe it was nine. But it definitely was not seven.)

"Girls," Wes said, frustration in his voice, "Three plus four… is…always…seven"—with extra emphasis on *always*.

For whatever reason, it was just one of those funny little moments you know you'll always remember. Perhaps it was because of the way Wes "pinged" every word of *is always seven*. Perhaps it was because time seemed to be suspended as we waited on the girls' answer. Or maybe we remember the moment because of how silly it is to get so frustrated over something so simple (and each of us does that).

As every mother reading this book knows, Wes's frustration had nothing to do with how much he loved the girls. He adored them—and still does. His frustration had to do with the fact that we'd gone over three plus four with them probably a hundred times, yet it still stymied them.

Now here are some questions we'd like to ask you: What aspect of your marriage seems to throw you every single time? What recurring incident seems to drive you to insanity whenever it happens?

Maybe, like me (Connie) you feel tension flush over your entire body. Maybe you grit your teeth. I don't know whether I do this because of the tension or because I don't want to say anything I'll later regret. But I feel instantly on edge.

Or maybe like me (Nancy), you feel as if the wind is instantly taken out of your sails, and you retreat into a little black hole for a time. Or perhaps you become instantly angry.

What does your husband do—or not do—that causes this reaction in you? Leave his clothes strewn about? Fail to help more with the kids? Say he'll do something but never gets around to it? Embarrass you in front of others? Consistently ignore your counsel? Never plan a special night out for the two of you—or if he does, it's all about something he likes to do? (Back when you were dating, you probably acted as if you enjoyed that activity too, which could be what he's remembering.)

Think for a moment and come up with one behavior that stymies you time and again. Most likely, you've come up with more than one, but for the time being, choose just one item from your mental list.

Here's our challenge to you: Would you be willing to mentally wipe away one of your husband's behaviors that irritates you? Whenever it popped up, would you be willing to train yourself to just let it go?

We're not suggesting you pick something he does that's harmful, such as alcoholism, abuse, pornography, or reckless spending. These are serious issues, and we recommend that you seek help. What we're asking you to choose is an irritant, not a lifestyle issue. You can choose the smallest thing—it doesn't matter.

Be warned, though! What we're really trying to do is not just help you give up reacting to that one thing. That "one thing" is the vessel we're using to help you accomplish something far more powerful, more poignant. In reality, we're asking you to do something far bigger than letting go of your negative response to one of your husband's annoying habits. (We'll talk more about this goal in the next chapter.)

I (Connie) want to tell you about a time in my marriage when the relationship was so cold, that if someone challenged me to give up reacting to something Wes did that irritated me, I'd have first listed about three hundred and fifty things from which to choose. Practically everything he did irritated me. And everything he didn't do irritated me even more. This fact isn't something I'm proud of. In fact, I'm horrified anew as I sit here at my computer in the early morning hours and see the words being typed out before me…by my own hands. I blink back tears as I think about those awful times.

Let me just say right now that if you're in just such an awful time in your marriage, be encouraged. It *will* pass. It only seems like it never will.

Anyway, I was the one who ushered in this awful season when I concluded that I was trying far harder than Wes in our marriage and that, until he upped his efforts, I was going to hold back my own. This was neither a smart nor a virtuous move. I naively thought I'd slip my marriage transmission into neutral gear. What I didn't know is that marriage transmissions don't have neutral gears. You're either going forward or you're going backward.

To stop trying is to go backward. To wait on your husband to catch up with you is to go backward. To think you've done more than your share is to go backward. And maybe your husband is moving backward too. But even if he is, the last thing you want to do is join him on that road. Why should both of you head down a dead-end road? One spouse needs to keep his or her senses and follow the compass in the right direction.

Back then I didn't grasp this fact. I just figured Wes would sooner or later figure out what was going on in our relationship and kick up his efforts a notch. But he didn't catch on at all. For one thing, his life was packed and stressful. He was working really long hours and trying to study on the side. Meanwhile our infant twin daughters were crying constantly.

So my husband was working round the clock, my daughters were crying round the clock, and I was irritated—with Wes— round the clock. It was mass misery.

When Wes did make an effort to connect with me, I cut him little slack. Before long, though, he quit trying. We simply existed. This awful season lasted for months. There wasn't screaming, yelling, threats to leave, or anything like that. In fact, we did pretty well at covering up to the world what was really going on. But, in reality, our marriage was about as warm as a block of ice.

Then came a time when I got into a Bible study led by Nancy. She taught seventeen of us what our job descriptions were as wives. Every week she spoke about what being a godly wife looked like. Every week I was more and more shocked to discover I wasn't quite as right as I'd led myself to believe. God was convicting me to begin changing—regardless of what Wes did or didn't do. What was up with that?

One of the first ways I began to change was to do exactly what we've just challenged you to do—to let go of reacting to something Wes did that irritated me. Well, he could never remember to take out the trash on Tuesdays, and for whatever reason, this grated on my nerves. I decided, though, that all this wasted energy could be put to better use. I determined to stop being irritated with his trash amnesia.

What I did was fairly simple. Instead of thinking of the task as Wes's job, I mentally delegated this job to myself. I didn't say anything to Wes, such as, "Hey, since your performance in this area is so poor, from now on I'll do it myself." I simply began carrying the garbage cans to the curb every Tuesday morning. Wes never said anything, and I'm not sure he even noticed. It didn't really matter. I'd decided to improve my own behavior and stop obsessing about his.

I wanted the awful time in our marriage to end. Taking out the trash myself was a small way of trying to make that happen. I could have spent the better part of my life being obsessed about the garbage, but it no longer seemed a worthy pursuit.

At first I found myself muttering all the way to the curb, "He should be doing this." These words seemed to defeat the point of what I was trying to do, so I set my thoughts in a new direction. When the next Tuesday rolled around and I carried the containers to the curb, I thanked God for two legs that worked…two arms that were strong…a brain that could remember when the trash collectors came…enough money to spend in order to have trash to fill the containers…a country to live in that provided trash pickup services…and on and on.

This may seem silly, but it's what I did. Initially I forced myself to do it just to keep from muttering to myself. But what I was doing, without even knowing it, was resetting my mind.

Eventually Tuesdays became a sort of Thanksgiving Day for me. I found myself looking up at the early morning sky and saying, "Good morning, God." I sometimes stood in the quiet of the day—out in the middle of the street—and took in the world around me. Sometimes the sun was popping through the clouds, or sometimes snow was beginning to fall. Often, an older neighbor would be taking his trash out at the same time I did, and we'd chat for a few minutes. Sometimes I was in such a hurry I didn't do any of these things, but usually I did. Regardless, I quit hanging the trash over my husband's head.

Amazingly, Wes now remembers—more often than he ever has before—to take out the trash. He still forgets more than he remembers, but he remembers more than he used to. It's not that his life has slowed down, because it hasn't. So I sometimes wonder if Wes's occasional remembering is God's way of telling me, "I'm noticing your efforts!" Once I wiped the trash irritant off my list, I decided to pick another one…and then another. As you get older, you realize how few things are really worthy of staying on the list. So when I notice something has landed there, I attempt to let it go. Or if it's a big enough deal, I talk to Wes about it and we work it out.

I recently heard about a woman who'd been happily married for sixty years. Someone asked her what her secret to a happy marriage was. She said that on her wedding day, she decided to make a list of ten things her new husband might do that could possibly irritate her—and then decided that these ten things would be exempt from causing her any irritation. She said it worked wonders for her marriage.

Of course, the person then asked this woman what those ten things were. The woman gave a gentle smile. She'd never gotten around to actually making the list of specifics, she said, but whenever her husband did something that irritated her, she told herself that surely that particular irritant would have been on her list. And then she let go of it.

Are you willing to let go of one thing your husband does that irritates you? If you're not, would you be willing to ask God to make you willing? Life's far too short to live by the wrong list.

My daughters finally learned that three plus four is always seven. It took me much longer to learn that my husband needs and deserves my grace on a daily basis.

BOTTOM LINE

*Three plus four is always seven,
and you plus God is always everything.*

Choose Discipline

Recently I (Connie) realized I'm at a point in my life where I need to lose some weight. I've struggled with this ever since our twins were born. Perhaps it was because—before I had children—I'd always found it hard to believe that women should ever struggle to lose their baby weight. In my young, know-it-all mind, I saw no reason a woman couldn't lose this weight within three months after the baby's birth.

Then I had a baby. In fact, I had two at once. My twins are now twenty-three years old, and I'm still struggling to lose my baby weight. I lost most of it five years ago, but somehow most of it managed to find me again.

So here I am, in the wee hours of a Sunday morning, sitting down to write a bit. My husband is at a conference in New Orleans. Two of my daughters are away at school. One of my daughters, Cassidy, is home to attend a friend's wedding.

While she was at the wedding last night, I went shopping at Sam's Club. I have a bridal shower to attend this afternoon, and for the bride-to-be I bought a crystal vase with the word *Love* etched on it. On my way home, I decided it would be fun to fill the vase with chocolates, so I made a U-turn and headed back to the store. Consciously, I was thinking the bulk size from Sam's would be far less expensive than buying the chocolate at a regular grocery store. Subconsciously, though, I was thinking that if I bought a huge bag of it, there would be plenty of chocolates left over for me.

You see, I never met a piece of chocolate I didn't like. I *love* chocolate.

Before I even got to the checkout counter, I'd torn open a corner of the bag and was chomping on the chocolates as I shopped for a few more things. I checked out, walked to my car, and unloaded everything out of the cart into the back of my car—except for the chocolate. It had a place of honor in the front seat, right beside me. I ate chocolate all the way home. I had so many empty wrappers, I poured out the rest of my soda at a stoplight so I could use the cup as a trash receptacle.

After I got home, I filled the vase with chocolate, and to my delight, there was still a whole lot left in the bag. I put away everything I'd bought—except the bag of chocolate. I left it lying on the counter for easy access.

My daughter called from the wedding reception. She was

having a grand time, and it would be a while before she got home. So I plopped in front of the television and had more chocolate.

My daughter got home around eleven and filled me in on the wedding details. Then we went to bed.

I awoke at five thirty the next morning and slipped downstairs to write. I rounded the counter to head into the study— and "what to my wondering eyes did appear?" You guessed it. There in all its glory was the bulk bag of chocolate. I tossed a few more pieces into my mouth...then a few more...then a few more. It's a wonder my stomach wasn't in complete rebellion at this point, but over the years it has developed an extremely high tolerance for massive amounts of chocolate.

I was practically making myself dizzy, going from the computer to the kitchen for more chocolate and then back to the computer. I refused to put the bag on my desk. I was afraid I would eat too much. (Hello!)

About thirty minutes into this insanity, I found myself standing in the kitchen with a green-foil-wrapped piece of chocolate in my hand. I started to unwrap it. As I did so, I told myself, *I'll eat just one more piece, then I'll stop.* After all, I did want to lose a little weight before Christmas.

Then it hit me. If I were going to lose weight, I was going to have to stop eating chocolate by the bulk-sized bag.

Something reverberated deep inside of me. I was sick of

living like this. I was sick of my penchant for chocolate being out of control. When was the next piece going to be my last?

I looked at that piece of half-opened chocolate for a few moments. I had two choices. I could either put it in my mouth… or wrap it back up and leave it alone. It was a poignant moment. Chocolate has been such a feel-good friend to me.

There I stood…in the middle of my kitchen…at five thirty in the morning…with a decision to make. I thought about what I was doing, and I thought about what I wanted to achieve. To put it simply, the two couldn't coexist. I couldn't eat chocolate to my heart's content *and* lose weight at the same time.

So I made a decision. I took the half-opened piece of candy and gently wrapped the foil back around it. Then I set that piece of chocolate on a shelf in my kitchen as a gentle reminder that if I wanted to reach my goal, I had to make choices to help me reach it. This effort is called discipline.

At the heart of every chapter in this book lies a nugget of truth you can incorporate into your life, a special something that will hopefully encourage your husband to listen to you. But making these life changes is going to require discipline. So if you want to…

- stop nagging
- understand your husband's way of communicating
- stop trying to make him into someone he isn't
- accept him as he is

- train yourself to begin noticing what he does right
- invest in his life
- greet him warmly whenever he comes home
- forgive him when he hurts your feelings
- and so on

…then you're going to have to choose the discipline of discipline.

And if I'm to lose weight, I need to guard (discipline) what I put into my mouth. If I'm going to become a righteous wife, I need to guard (discipline) what comes out of my mouth.

Discipline isn't one of our favorite words, is it? We far prefer *fun* and *carefree*. However, anytime we set our eyes on a goal—be it losing weight or becoming a virtuous, glorious woman—it isn't "fun" or "carefree" that keeps us moving down the path toward the prize. It's discipline.

Old habits die hard. They're hard to break and even harder to keep broken. Your old way of thinking will lure you when you least expect it. But when it does, take every thought captive and refuse to yield to temptation's shallow promises (see 2 Corinthians 10:5). To help you stay on track—at least initially—picking something to represent discipline in your life can be helpful. For me, it's that piece of candy wrapped in green foil. Choose your own symbol…something to remind you, every time you see it, of the day you decided to choose the discipline of discipline.

Choose today to discipline yourself to become a wonderful

wife. Leave your husband to God. God is big enough to change him, and He's working His purpose out in His own timing.

BOTTOM LINE

*A journey of a thousand miles
begins with a single step.*

21

A Marriage Thermometer

When you were dating, your husband-to-be understood and responded to your body language. You tossed your hair, listened to him with rapt attention, laughed at his stories, and flirted with him. You were irresistible!

During this courtship phase, your husband would read these signs like a hunter reading deer tracks. Now that you're married, your husband has "bagged his dear" and doesn't have to work so hard at reading signs.

Allan Pease, coauthor with his wife, Barbara, of *The Definitive Book of Body Language,* explains that men are really pretty basic and can't pick up on the constant flow of nonverbal signals that women give. And since so much of our communication is nonverbal, those signals are often more important than what we say.

Research by psychologist Albert Mehrabian, in his *Nonverbal Communication,* supports that it's not what you say but how you say it that really matters. For example, if you're walking together, Mehrabian says the following are signs that the two of you are in sync:

- walking at about the same pace
- walking side by side
- holding hands or occasionally touching
- making eye contact

And these would be signs that you're out of sync:

- one partner walking far ahead (which may indicate a wish to lead or a low comfort level with the partner)
- walking far behind (indicating a level of fear or intimidation)

And if you're sitting together, Mehrabian observes, these are in-sync signs:

- bodies angled toward each other
- facing each other
- making eye contact
- engaging in conversation

The absence of these behaviors signals that you're out of sync.

Dr. Mehrabian describes other warning signs as well, such as stiffness in the shoulders and neck, which can indicate coldness and anxiety. Eye contact, he continues, is one of the biggest indicators of relationship. Both partners should be able to freely look into each other's eyes during their interactions, including sex.

"Now what," you may be asking, "am I supposed to do with this information?"

If you and your husband are really good at connecting and these indicators of good rapport describe you two, that's great! If, however, these items don't characterize your relationship, all is not lost. Just as we recognize a fever as a sign to take proactive measures to get healthy again, so too we can see our body language indicating an emotional and/or physical disconnect within our marriage and can take steps to reestablish the connection.

We'll examine a plan for this in the next chapter.

BOTTOM LINE

Do your eyes...as well as your lips...say
"I love you" to your husband?

22

RECONNECTing

As women, we tend to be at least three times more likely than our husbands to pick up on nonverbal cues of body language. Being able to read these cues is a gift.

If your marriage is exhibiting indicators of emotional disconnection, there are things you can do to reconnect. Your effort may take time and patience, because what developed over time (perhaps over years) isn't going to be changed in a day. Relationships, like houses, need maintenance. Sometimes they even need extreme makeovers. And because nobody's perfect, your marriage will show wear from emotional meltdowns, communication problems, and plain old mistakes. You need to become good at recovering, recuperating, and reconnecting.

To help in the process, consider the following suggestions for getting your relationship back on solid ground. To aid our memories in retaining these suggestions, we're using the acronym RECONNECT.

RECONNECT: RECOVER YOUR EARLY LOVE

Have you walked away from your first love for your husband? If so, just as Revelation 2:5 (MSG) encourages the church at Ephesus to, "Turn back! Recover your dear early love," we encourage you to turn back and recover that first love you had for your husband.

rEconnect: ENCOURAGE

Be encouraging to your husband. A man who hears encouragement from his wife will run, not walk, to listen to what she has to say to him.

Make encouragement your habit. Begin small, if need be. Be sincere, not an empty flatterer. This is a must. A man knows when he's being patronized.

Those bearing good news are always welcomed. (In ancient times, a bearer of bad news was often shot!) So bring good news habitually, and you'll be habitually welcomed—and generally listened to.

reCONNECT: CONNECT

If you're out of the habit of physical touch, begin again. Touch lowers blood pressure and reestablishes a sense of intimacy.

Gently touch his hand when you join him over coffee.

Scratch or rub his back. My husband, Ray, loves it when I cut his hair, because it involves a lot of touching of his head, neck, and shoulders.

Touch can speak volumes, and it's a language most men love. My sister Christine never parts from her husband Carl (even to run an errand) without giving him a hug. He's begun the same practice with her. "I'm going to run to the bank," he'll say. "Come get your hug."

recOnnect: Overlook Offenses

It's all too easy to become thin skinned, especially since we women can remember offenses that date as far back as our courting days. And when we're angry, we tend to throw into the mix everything our husbands have ever done "wrong." What we stir up is almost like a cauldron of evil potions. Our actions in this regard can cause hard feelings and hurt that last for days.

Learn to place a higher priority on relationship than winning an argument. Don't sweat the small stuff.

Consider the wisdom in this little poem (author unknown):

> To keep a marriage brimming
> with love in the loving cup—
> When you're wrong, admit it;
> and when you're right, shut up!

recoNnect: Notice the Positives

When your husband experiences success in any area, share his pride. Let him know you're proud of him, especially when the accomplishments are important to him.

Several years ago, my husband, Ray, was honored by his graduating class and inducted into their hall of fame. He was rightly proud of the tribute, and his award sits in a place of honor in our home. We continue to share things we remember that made the day so special.

Notice your husband's positives traits, as well as his accomplishments—and express your appreciation to him for those characteristics. If you really want to see him listening to you intently, let him know that you're very aware of and thankful for his achievements and good qualities.

reconNect: Never Refuse to Make
or Accept an Apology

First, never refuse to make an apology when the fault lies with you. Let's say there's been a quarrel, and an emotional meltdown resulted. If you were at fault—if you made a nonissue into a major issue, if you fueled the fire rather than helped put it out— tell your husband you're sorry.

As for accepting his apology, realize that many husbands find saying the words "I'm sorry" as difficult to utter as asking for directions when they're lost. Accept your husband's wordless apology in the form of flowers, a tender card, or even a gentle pat on your bottom. Make it a personal rule to never rebuff your husband's outward demonstration of affection or apology.

RECONNEct: ENJOY EACH OTHER

Next to love, we can't think of anything that brings more joy into a home than laughter. Not laughter at someone's expense, but the habitual, lighthearted celebration of the funny side of things.

In surveys of happy marriages and even on lists of qualities that unmarried people are looking for in a mate, one of the traits high on the list is a good sense of humor. This quality is scriptural as well: "A cheerful heart is good medicine" (Proverbs 17:22). So cultivate lightheartedness. You'll be glad every time you laugh over an irritation or criticism rather than escalate it into an argument. A friend shared her experience in this area, saying,

> My husband is really good at making a funny when
> we have a minor disagreement. Early in our marriage
> I would get offended by his teasing and push him into
> a fight. Needless to say, my sour response made us mis-
> erable and wasn't good for our relationship. Because I
> struggled to let go of the small stuff, I finally asked God
> to give me a less serious outlook. Now, most of the time,
> I relent and laugh.

reconneCt: Create a Safe Place

Your home should be a safe haven for you both, not an environment of additional stress. If life around the house is strained, especially if one of you is near a meltdown point, don't complicate the problem by confronting your husband. Instead, give each other some space. Doing so gives you both room to cool off and opens up space for God to quietly work in both your hearts.

One good thing to do during those tense times is the grocery shopping. Yes, we're serious. Don't storm out in anger, saying, "You're always in a bad mood. I've got to get away for a while." Simply say, "I'm going out for some groceries. Can you think of anything we need?" Even the choice of the pronoun *we* is a subtle reaffirmation of your relationship.

If your husband is the one who decides to escape, allow him a safe place to calm down in peace—the garage, the tennis court, the golf course, a backyard hammock, any place that helps him mentally and emotionally regroup.

reconnecT: Together in Christ

Remember Jesus's first miracle? It happened at a wedding feast (see John 2:1–11). When He was asked in faith, He miraculously supplied what had run out in the marriage feast.

You may feel that you have run out of something in your marriage. If so, why not extend to Jesus a wedding invitation?

Right now. Pray that He'll enter into your own marriage to sup-
ply whatever you've run out of. Perhaps it's the main ingredi-
ent—love. Perhaps it's respect, or joy, or even sexual intimacy.

The Lord is able to provide whatever's missing: "My God
will meet all your needs according to his glorious riches in Christ
Jesus" (Philippians 4:19).

BOTTOM LINE

*When something electrical becomes
disconnected from its power source,
you stop and reconnect it. How
much more important is
reconnecting in your marriage!*

23

CIRCULAR THINKING

"NAN, ARE YOU GOING TO be doing the wash today?"

"Yes, honey."

"I'll bring it down."

I then took the laundry to the washroom and divided it into four piles—two piles of whites for bleaching, one light colored not requiring bleach, and a dark load. When Ray came home from work, after greeting me, he asked, "Did you do the wash?"

"Yes!" I replied. "All four loads, *and* I put them away. How was your day?"

"Four loads?" he responded. "There weren't four loads. There was only one!"

"Well, actually, there was some wash already in the hamper, so it turned into four loads."

"No, there weren't four loads. There was only one!"

"Well, the point is, Ray, the laundry's done, folded, and put away."

"No, the point is, *there was only one load.*"

By now I was a bit exasperated. I asked him if he had a problem with the amount of soap or water I'd used. That wasn't the issue at all. Ray's issue was, there was only one load of wash.

Our evening went on uneventfully, but the next morning as I was driving to work, I started to mull this over. I thought, *Maybe he should do his own wash. Then he'd be sure to get the load count correct. Doesn't he realize I've washed thousands and thousands of loads of laundry over the years?* On and on my thoughts went. I was fixated on this perplexing event.

Then, annoyed with myself for even going there, I asked the Lord to spring-clean my mind from the clutter of last night's ridiculous problem.

Then this thought came to me: *Your thinking is circular. It should be linear.*

I was shocked. *That's exactly right,* I told myself. *I do this all the time. I rehash things needlessly.*

Do you?

What a waste of time. What difference did it make who was right about the number of loads and who was wrong? It wasn't as if Ray had shot our dog. Ours really was a silly disagreement. Immediately, I felt spring-cleaned.

If you want to have a warm relationship with your husband, why insist on proving your point? Why insist on always being right? Men don't like this. Who does? Why not just drop the subject? You may later discover he'd had a difficult day, and his argument over the number of wash loads had nothing at all to do with you.

The fact of the matter is that Ray and I have had many difficult days since Valentine's Day 2006, when he was diagnosed with stage-four cancer of the lungs, kidneys, and liver. He's valiantly fighting for his very life. He's been in and out of the hospital facing chemotherapy, CAT scans, bad news, extreme weakness, and an uncertain future. Perhaps the wash-day incident was helpful to him. It certainly got his mind off his serious health problem, and if that's what was needed, it was worth it.

The bigger issue in God's economy, I'm certain, is that I get the lesson about circular thinking. Rehashing past events over and over is a complete waste of time for me.

And for you, too.

BOTTOM LINE

Think linear! Going round and round will only make you dizzy—and mad.

GIVING RESPECT

ISN'T IT SO LIKE GOD? He charges a husband and wife with the responsibility of giving each other the one thing that's hardest for each of them not only to give but also to keep giving. In general, a man would rather be respected than loved. And a woman would rather be loved than respected. So God commands husbands to love their wives and wives to respect their husbands. God doesn't do this to frustrate us, but to refine our characters.

A man shouldn't have to jump through hoops to get his wife to respect him. It's due him because of his title: husband. "And the wife must see to it that she respects her *husband*" (Ephesians 5:33, NASB). Respect is the special esteem or consideration we hold for another person or thing.

This means you show respect for your husband by highly regarding him. Do you withhold respect from your husband because you don't feel he deserves it? So many women think their husbands have to earn their respect, but if you notice the wording of that verse in Ephesians, nowhere does it mention the earning aspect.

But practically speaking, how is this respect demonstrated? Let's think through some ways you perhaps haven't considered lately:

- Does your husband know he's first on your earthly priority list? What do you say or do to communicate this?
- Do the children hear you speaking respectfully *to* and *about* their dad?
- Has your husband ever heard you say, "I never knew I could love anyone the way I love you"?
- Do you honor his decisions?
- If someone asked your husband, would he say that you respect him?

In 1990 the company Ray worked for was sold. He was the president, but not the owner. The new owners came in with their own president. Needless to say, being replaced was a blow to Ray.

Every day he dressed in his business suit and tie and went out to look for a new position. One day he came home saying something I'd never heard from him before: "The Lord said to me, 'Your job is not in this city. Make two phone calls.' "

He did, and both companies wanted him. He flew to Omaha (we were living in North Carolina), and he was hired...which of course meant I would move as well.

Did I want to move? No! Our children were in North Carolina, I had a wonderful ministry there, and my father lived nearby. And for those of you who don't live in Omaha, have you ever said, "Let's go to Omaha for a vacation"?

Ray had been hit hard in an area of great importance to a man: his self-esteem, as an excellent and respected executive in his lifelong field of expertise. He was further wounded by his difficult choice to move away from children he loved and from a home he loved in a beautiful community where he was known and respected.

So I made the conscious choice to do all I could during this time to be his helper. I chose to pour myself into him so he could heal and regain his self-esteem. I intentionally loved and supported him day after day.

And guess what? Our years in Omaha (all fifteen of them) have been the best times of our lives. I've lived in numerous places in the world, but I have come to love Omaha the best. It's the result of God's grace. I'm glad I respected my husband and his decision.

Do you respect your husband and his decisions? You never know what doors might open when you choose to follow God's directives for your life. For instance, I don't believe I would have written books or had my current ministry if back then I'd talked Ray out of doing what he felt was best to do.

Perhaps today is the day for you to begin respecting your husband in a fresh way. Here are a few suggestions:

- Admire him in public.
- Kiss him lovingly as you part for the workday.
- Thank him for working so hard for you and your family.
- Tell him how great he looks.
- Admire his sexual abilities.
- Make an effort to look nice for him.

If your doctor prescribed a certain medicine for your physical health, you'd take it, wouldn't you? Of course. Why? Because you trust him to know best what to do.

Well, God Almighty has told you to respect your husband. What are you going to do with this prescription for your marital health?

BOTTOM LINE

*Respect is to a man what
love is to a woman.*

What Your
Disrespect Triggers

A WOMAN'S NUMBER ONE NEED in marriage is to feel loved. Study after study confirms this, and we women aren't surprised at the result. But, as we noted in the previous chapter, feeling loved isn't the number one need in a man's life. In fact, feeling loved ranks way down on the list of what's important to men.

Instead, studies reveal two things that vie for the number one position on the list of what a man needs most in his marriage: sexual fulfillment and respect. Some research places respect first, while other studies place sexual fulfillment first. It's back and forth, right down the line. But for a woman, there's no such inconsistency. Nothing comes close to her desire to feel loved by her husband.

Because her desire to be loved is so intense, a woman nearly always assumes that feeling loved must have the same priority in her husband's life as well. So she'll set about trying to do for her husband what she wishes he would do for her: make him feel like he is the most loved man on the face of this earth. Her efforts aren't wasted, certainly, but they probably aren't having nearly the impact she'd like to think. Because what a guy really wants is respect and sexual fulfillment. These comprise his mother tongue.

Likewise, since guys have a strong need for respect and sexual fulfillment, they think we women want the same things. So they set about trying to give them to us. They go to work, mow the lawn, fix the leaky faucet, and do all sorts of other things. Taking care of us like this is their way of showing us respect. However, such efforts may go largely unnoticed, because the wife is longing for him to hold her in his arms and look into her eyes—at least occasionally—and tell her he loves her and would marry her all over again.

Furthermore, when a guy goes about trying to give his wife the other thing he so longs for—sexual fulfillment—he's shocked to discover she's not exactly leaping for joy at his overtures. He doesn't get this. At all. He's completely puzzled, not to mention discouraged, deflated, and demeaned. He can't escape his own deep longing for sexual fulfillment. In fact, he would love for her to provide this for him every night. And he assumes she has the same deep need. What a husband doesn't realize is that if his wife isn't feeling loved and cherished, she has about as much interest in sex as volunteering to have her hair pulled out with tweezers.

In their book *Motivating Your Man God's Way,* Emerson and Sarah Eggerichs explain that when you as a wife feel unloved, you react negatively to your husband. You know you're being negative, but that's not the point here. What you probably don't realize is that your husband interprets your negative reaction as disrespectful, and this is a major disconnect. To you, your negative reaction is purely defensive. To your husband, you're coming across as offensive. You know you're crying out for love. You know you have good intentions. By your negative reaction, the code you're sending—which is obvious to all women—is "I feel unloved." Lamentably, your husband doesn't crack that code. He sees you as being on the attack, and he feels rejected. When you either rebuff or respond coldly to his sexual advances, he feels you're rejecting him. All too quickly, if this cycle isn't broken, you and your husband become two ships passing in the night.

By the way, we've been on these ships, and it bothered us greatly. Some days, though, we found we liked being on our own little ship—and that bothered us even more. And well it should. At these times we knew we had to address not only our negativity issues, but also whatever tempted us to go things alone.

One of the biggest mistakes a woman can make is to tell herself that she'll start respecting her husband when he begins loving her. We believe our husbands should love us unconditionally, but we don't feel we have to respect them in the same manner—unconditionally.

This is where we get off track. We're called to respect our

husbands in the same manner they're called to love us: without conditions. But women today have put a qualifier on the respect issue. We think our husbands must earn our respect—and this is wrong thinking.

"Wait a minute," you're probably saying. "What if he makes a poor financial decision, or insults my mother, or says something really stupid to the kids?"

Well, what if he does? No doubt he has, and he will again. Our tendency as women is to think this kind of behavior means our husbands don't merit our respect, so we wait for them to earn it back. This strategy is marital suicide, pure and simple.

After all, have you as a wife ever let your husband down? embarrassed him? made a comment that would have been better left unsaid? questioned his wisdom? rejected him sexually? forgotten to tell him something important? done something really foolish?

Yes—to all the above.

Now imagine if your husband decided to stop loving you because you did these things. You would be outraged, wouldn't you? Why? Because—as everyone knows—a man is *always* supposed to love his wife, no matter what. In fact, if you're spiritually inclined, you would even say he's to love you as Christ loved the church. Your foul-ups shouldn't make even the smallest dent in his love for you.

Yet somehow we conclude that each of our husbands' foul-ups is worthy of our loss of respect. Yes, while we would still say we love our husbands, we've made our respect conditional upon how they conduct themselves.

The *Motivating Your Man God's Way* authors go on to explain that the person in the marriage who's more mature is obligated to make the first move in these areas. Doing so will, in turn, motivate and energize the other person to fulfill his or her obligation. Each person has the power to initiate change in the marriage—the mature wife by respecting her husband, the mature husband by loving his wife. Clearly, there's no reason at all for you to wait for your husband's love to motivate your respect.

Remember, respect is what your husband craves and what motivates him to love you, especially during moments of conflict. And during such conflict, he isn't shutting down and withdrawing because he feels unloved. He never doubted your love. He's stonewalling because he feels a measure of your disdain for him, and he doesn't function well in the face of scorn. Actually, he needs reassurance of your respect, but he dares not ask for fear you'll readily say, "I don't respect you during episodes like this. You need to change!" This comment would be equivalent to his telling you, "I don't love you during episodes like this. You need to perform!" Such a message sends an arrow through a spouse's heart.

One of the greatest gifts you can give your husband is to respect him when he's having a bad day or making a decision you might not agree with. In fact, these are the times he needs your respect the most.

Your respect for your husband shouldn't be based on whether you feel like giving it or whether you feel he deserves it. Your respect is to be a gift he can count on day after day after day.

BOTTOM LINE

You can't put a price tag on love...and you shouldn't put one on respect either.

26

Two Ways to Spell Intimacy

Here's another interesting aspect of maleness: for most men, their sexual drives (unlike ours) rarely depend on whether their emotional tanks are filled. Wise is the woman who recognizes this and gives herself to her husband regardless of whether she feels he deserves it.

Too often we forget that physical intimacy with our husbands is often the kindling to cause a man to be more loving and attentive to his wife. If you ignore or neglect your mate's sexual needs, he'll have little desire to listen to you. A man whose wife meets his sexual needs will more likely meet his wife's need for loving communication. So, as someone once put it, "Don't say 'I do' at the altar but 'I don't' in the bedroom."

And on this topic, remember another difference in our general makeup: men are more visual, women more emotional. An attractive woman stirs a man, while a nurturing man stirs a woman. Your husband cares about how you look, and you should as well. You may like wearing old sweats and a baggy sweatshirt day after day, but your husband would prefer seeing you in something else. We're not talking stilettos and evening wear, but simply outfits that look and fit nicely.

Men consider their wives a reflection of themselves. If you take little care with your appearance, your husband may take this personally and feel frustrated, discouraged, and perhaps even angry. After all, this was of primary importance when you were wooing each other—and he had no idea this area would change after the wedding. Too often a wife considers her husband's desire for her to look nice as shallow and unreasonable, and she thinks, *It's his problem*. But that's foolishness. Accept your husband's God-given makeup, and be willing to dress for him.

BOTTOM LINE

*As Dr. Gary and Barbara Rosberg
(coauthors of The Five Love Needs of
Men and Women) once put it, both men
and women need intimacy. It's just that
women spell it t-a-l-k, while guys spell it
s-e-x. Neither is better; just different.*

27

Conflict Comes... but It Shouldn't Stay

During the past few years, Wes and I (Connie) were youth-group sponsors at our church. Every Sunday night, between fifty and sixty kids descended on our house and talked about everything from sporting events to battles with pornography and sex to salvation. We grew to love these kids tremendously.

The small group I shepherded included six young women who were high-school seniors. A few weeks before they headed off to college, we went out to dinner for a final time of being together. It was a special evening and one I'll always remember.

At one point the talk turned to dating, weddings, and marriage. One of the girls had been dating a young man for quite some time, and the others in the group began asking her questions about their relationship.

"What do you do when you have a fight?" one of them asked.

My young friend's eyes sparkled, and her face lit up with a huge smile. "That's an easy question," she replied. "Actually, we never fight. We're really compatible, and we just get along really well. It's unbelievable. We've never had a single fight in almost two years."

The others gasped in amazement. How romantic! To find someone you get along with all the time! The girls were quite impressed and said they hoped they would be that lucky when it came time to marry.

Their remarks reminded me of my own at that age, and I told them as much. I went into marriage thinking we would have very little, if any, conflict. My parents had always gotten along remarkably well, and I assumed Wes and I would too.

But I was extremely naive. What I didn't consider was the fact that my parents came from similar backgrounds and that their inherent temperaments were nearly identical as well. Even their love languages were the same. Wes and I, on the other hand, are almost polar opposites on every front. Our upbringings were different, our personalities are opposite, and so are our love languages. In the beginning, conflict was almost an everyday occurrence at our house.

The girls asked what kinds of things Wes and I had conflict over. I rattled off a list of things that included everything from how to squeeze the toothpaste to heavy theological issues. They were shocked. To hear that we'd struggled like this was extremely sobering to them. After all, we were pillars of the church. Their gaiety quickly turned to seriousness.

"Wow," one of the girls responded, taking in what I'd just said. "It's not exactly 'happily ever after,' is it?"

I leaned forward and spoke with such earnestness my voice broke.

"Listen to me, girls. Conflict doesn't mean you can't have 'happily ever after.' In fact, you won't have 'happily ever after' if you don't learn to work through conflict."

We spent the rest of the evening talking about this truth, and I hope that one day, when they find themselves battling with their husbands, they'll remember a bit of what we spoke of that night. I wish for them the same things I wish for my own daughters: I so want them to succeed in their marriages.

Some experts say the number one identifier in determining marital success is how a couple deals with conflict. Whenever conflict arose in the early years of our marriages, both of us handled it similarly: Words were exchanged, and we found we could generally out-talk, out-stubborn, and out-wait our husbands. Rarely was anything resolved. To us, every battle was a hill to die on. We didn't know how to let go of an issue—nor did we want to. Instead, we kept a running score in our minds of who was winning, and of course, we were always the victors. (How very sad.) Over the years, our pride and egos grew. One thing always mystified us, though: we were so unhappy. Perhaps this sounds familiar to you?

What do you suppose would happen if—in the midst of your next conflict—you were to take a U-turn? Instead of using harsh words, you choose soft ones. Instead of matching insult for insult, you respond with kindness. Your husband might well be shocked into silence. Could this approach be more productive? It certainly couldn't be less.

When we first began responding to conflict this way, our husbands were completely unprepared for our fresh approach. They were so baffled they didn't know what to say or do. They were so used to having to defend themselves against our harsh words that they didn't know how to react when the harsh words didn't come. It's sad to say, but they weren't used to being treated with dignity or respect when conflict arose. We had always gone immediately into fight mode—each person for himself. Now, however, when harsh words arise from one of husbands, he doesn't hear anything back. He only hears the fading echo of his own words. And it's hard for a person to argue with himself.

This new tactic was something we learned from Proverbs 15:1, a verse that tells us that harsh words stir up anger, while soft words turn anger away. We were amazed at how free we felt when we disengaged from our old ways.

What we had to learn—and what we're suggesting to you—

is to *respond* rather than *react*. There's a huge difference between the two. Reacting takes but a split second. It's a little like playing hot potato. You lob the verbal grenade back at your partner as fast as you can. Reacting doesn't think things through, and it doesn't care what damage will be incurred by one's choice of words. Reacting is all about winning, and words are used as weapons.

Responding takes but a few seconds more, and those are well-invested seconds. You see, responding takes the time to think through one's choice of words—realizing that once they're launched, they can't be taken back. Responding also recognizes that damage done in a few minutes can linger for months or even years. Learning to respond means maturity—the maturity to remember that your role as a godly wife is to respect your husband even when disagreements occur.

Let's say your husband comes home from work and decides he'd like a glass of milk before supper. He opens the refrigerator only to find there's no milk in sight. He's had a long day and he's tired. And he's probably not considering how *you* have had a long day and are tired as well. He's not overlooking your tiredness on purpose; he's simply focused on that glass of milk and annoyed not to find any.

"Is it too much to expect there to be milk in this house?" he asks, a bit sharply.

Here's where you can choose to either react or respond. It would be so easy to say, "Why is it always up to me to make sure we have milk? And bread. And fruit. And potatoes. And cereal. And clean laundry. And *everything else anybody wants*? You're a grown man. Surely it wouldn't kill you to buy a gallon of milk every now and then. Honestly! Why is it you always notice the negative and never comment on the positive? I've bought ten years' worth of milk—and you can buy it for the next ten years. Starting right now."

So much for a warm welcome home.

The alternate choice would be for you to hold your tongue, think things through for a moment, and then respond. You remind yourself that your husband is tired and hungry. He's not attacking you personally; he's probably thinking about something back at work. Or maybe he's worried about that house payment due next week. You just don't know.

A responding woman thinks all this through and then decides to choose her words carefully, realizing they'll set the tone for the rest of the evening. She's a noble woman traveling the high road.

So she takes a deep breath, looks at her husband, and says, "No, it's not too much to ask to have milk in the house. I hadn't even noticed it was gone. I'll get it first thing tomorrow. Could I make you a glass of iced tea or lemonade instead?"

When a woman chooses to respond instead of react, it almost always influences her husband. Her kind words often have a great effect on him. Perhaps they cause him to regret his own harshness without a word even being spoken. But when she chooses to react to his words with sharp words of her own, she sets in motion a downward spiral, marking the rest of the evening with tension and strife. In a nutshell, reacting unleashes the tongue and is self-centered, while responding holds the tongue and is other-centered.

Furthermore, being a party to escalating anger is an open invitation for chaos and ungodliness to rule your marriage. If you have small children, you're modeling for them behavior they shouldn't have to see, and years down the road it may come out in ways you can't imagine. One day you could well be the recipient of this same kind of talk from them. Or you may sow into your children poor relationship skills that will reap difficulties in their marriages. "We learned it from you, Mom," they'll say. What heartbreaking words! So take a hard look at yourself and ask God to help you see any areas that need to be changed.

If your kids are older and you think it's too late, be encouraged. I (Nancy) was in my forties, and my children were in their late teens and early twenties, when I began to change in this area. Now my kids tell me they can't remember those times when I wasn't respectful toward their dad. This is nothing short of miraculous. It's as if they've experienced some kind of spiritual amnesia.

As you begin changing your behavior and as the years go by, something similar could well occur with your adult children. If you persevere, somehow the present seems to color over the past. I sometimes wonder if this might be God's way of saying He takes note of changed hearts and erases many of those sad, destructive memories we create in our children.

Remember, conflict isn't a sign of an unhealthy marriage. It's simply a reality of every marriage relationship. But if conflict is not dealt with in a healthy manner, the fallout can linger for days. And husbands who are living with fallout aren't usually in listening mode.

Here are a few points to remember:

- When conflict is handled correctly, it can actually cause you to feel closer as a couple.
- Don't react and immediately speak the first words that come to your mind.
- Stop and consider the effect your words will have on the relationship—and *then* respond.
- If your husband is the one reacting, overlook it. The last thing he needs from you at that point is a lecture on his poor choice of words.
- Consider discussing certain things at a later time when emotions have calmed.
- Don't automatically assume you're right. At the very least, acknowledge his point of view.
- If you've reacted in a wrong way, apologize.
- If your husband apologizes for a wrong attitude, accept his apology—and even go a step further by letting him know how much you appreciate it. (It's often harder for men to say they're sorry than it is for women.)

Even if you feel certain your husband is in the wrong, don't press him for an apology either directly (with words) or indirectly (by pouting or withdrawing). Remember, his response is an issue between God and him.

Conflict is a part of every close relationship, but it shouldn't be allowed to linger or fester. If you want warm communication with your husband, learning to respond appropriately to conflict is one of the best defenses against a cold, barren marriage.

BOTTOM LINE

Responding—not reacting—is the key to "happily ever after."

28

A GENTLE RESPONSE

WHEN YOU READ THE WORDS, *No more tit-for-tat living,* what comes to mind? Do you automatically think, *If someone speaks harshly to me, don't I have every right to retaliate?* Or, *Isn't holding my tongue acting like a doormat and flinging open the door to being treated poorly the rest of my life?*

Not in God's economy. It has just the opposite effect, although you may not see it at first.

God's perspective is very different from the world's. In fact, living God's way of turning the other cheek and not retaliating has a surprising effect on those who may be braced for our attack, but I'm getting ahead of myself.

Let us ask, is God's way hard to live out? Yes.

Do husbands respond differently to wives who adopt this way of life? Are you kidding? Of course they do.

Are they skeptical about the apparent change of heart? Absolutely!

Do some men try to aggravate their wives just to test them? Lots of times.

So is it worth trying to live this way? Well, what do you think? Or, as Dr. Phil might say, "How's your present behavior working for you? Is it drawing you closer to your husband or pushing you further apart?"

Another question for you: what does God have to say about words? Plenty. Let's listen again to a truth given to us by the Inventor of languages: "A gentle response defuses anger" (Proverbs 15:1, MSG).

Gentle words *defuse* anger? How does that work? In a word, well! Consider what happened just this morning when my husband and I (Nancy) left for work at the same time…

We have a one-car garage that, like our house, was built in 1921. We also have a one-car driveway. I started my car, then waited for Ray to pull out behind me so I could back out. And I waited and waited.

Finally Ray opened his car door and stepped out. He wasn't happy. We just put a new starter in the car last week, but now it wouldn't start. He phoned the auto repair shop and told them to come *right* over. I called my office and informed them I'd be late.

The waiting time for the tow truck dragged on. Ray was steamed.

I suggested that after his car was towed, he could take my car to work. I sprinkled my suggestion with gentle words like *honey* and *dear*. I also told him I could call my office and let them know I'd spend the day at home on a work-related project.

Ray calmed down. His frustration was defused. The tow truck came and took away his car. And Ray went off in mine.

Now what if I'd responded differently to Ray's irritation? "Why can't you use a repair shop that fixes it right the first time?" Or, "I really don't appreciate having to wait for you like this." Such harsh words only stir up anger. Gentle words turn anger away.

The next verse in Proverbs 15 says this: "Knowledge flows like spring water from the wise; fools are leaky faucets, dripping nonsense." If I'd reacted by simply expressing my own irritation, I would have been dripping nonsense.

The next verse states a most amazing fact: "GOD doesn't miss a thing—he's alert to good and evil alike." If you think no one notices what is said in such a situation, you're wrong. You're being watched all the time. God Himself hears everything that you say. Isn't that a sobering thought?

Does this mean we can't speak the truth to our husbands in love? Not at all! But we've found that waiting a bit causes most husbands to listen to what we have to say, because then we aren't acting out of anger to an already annoyed person. As verse 4 says, "Kind words heal and help."

By living this way, you become an anger defuser because you're saying nothing to inflame an already heated situation. You're also causing the atmosphere to change for the better. If

you let a little time go by, your husband's focus will change...
and he'll enjoy listening to his very friendly wife.

So here's the challenge for you: Try deliberately giving up tit-for-tat living for three weeks in a row. If you blow it, start over.

As you train yourself to choose gentle words, you'll find a strange thing happening: you are the one who'll feel better. And, perhaps even stranger, your husband may stop turning deaf ears toward everything you say.

BOTTOM LINE

*The only last word you should
try to get in is a kind one.*

29

CHOOSE WORDS
WITH CARE

WHILE PREPARING FOR THIS CHAPTER, we did an Internet word search. We typed in "choose words with care." The results were sixty-three million sites to choose from. We were pleased to see that this topic was considered important by so many.

But then we began reading through the first few sites. To our dismay, they were all about smart-speak and current hot-button words designed to aid in generating greater profit: "You're on your way to identifying the key words and phrases most likely to drive targeted traffic to your site." Our search results were *not* about interacting with wisdom in relationships.

How could this be? Are we as a nation so prosperity driven that we care more about financial gain than maintaining and nurturing relationships?

Among so many other accomplishments, Benjamin Franklin was also our first ambassador to France. He was known for the fine art of diplomacy, of the judicious choice of soft words. It has been said that when presenting someone with a new way of looking at an issue, he would use this phrase: "I invite you to consider…" This is a wonderful example of a soft-power introduction for an idea that might be met with resistance.

My (Nancy's) sister Christine began to use this soft-power approach in her marriage. Her intent was to choose her words carefully and avoid controversy. She discovered, however, that in her zeal to avoid controversy (which isn't always easy with a plain-spoken husband), she sometimes pressed and transgressed the boundaries of integrity.

As women, we often use soft words in our interactions with our husbands. But if we use them without integrity, our soft words too easily become manipulative. We can fall into the trap of gentle deceit, using words to get our way. Soft words minus integrity equals manipulation. For example, in all apparent innocence, the wife might enter the room wearing a new blouse.

Husband: "Is that a new blouse?"

Wife: "Not really. I've had it for a while."

Christine had expected Carl to ask that question—and she'd prepared that response, which was really a rationalization. She'd had the blouse only since the previous Saturday.

When we choose words carefully like this, we tell ourselves

we're not being deceitful. Last Saturday, after all, was "a while" ago. Besides, we deserve something new. And his suits cost much more than a blouse anyway.

But the reality is, if we're not being 100 percent honest, we're being dishonest. So ask yourself these questions: *Am I being straight with my husband? Would I be able to answer, "Yes, it's a new blouse"?*

Could it be that one of the reasons your husband doesn't listen much is because in conversations with you, your antenna is up, you're alert for possible issues, and you bob and weave with words to avoid conversations about such hot-button issues as how much money you're spending?

At one point I (Nancy) actually boasted of this skill that I call octopusing. When an octopus is threatened, it expels ink to cloud the water so it can make its escape. Though I am no longer proud of it, at times I have used words to cloud the water, not to clarify.

Remember, a man asks questions to gather information. By answering so misleadingly, I'm thwarting his attempt.

Now let's talk about "hard power." Sometimes in our responses to our husbands' words or deeds we step over the line into emotional anger. Hard power that works through coercion and threats then comes into play. We use angry words, insults, tears, and the withholding of sexual favors or emotional intimacy. The gloves come off, and we rehash his list of prior offenses.

Hard power breaks down relationships, and it can destroy weeks of loving interaction almost instantly.

The weapons in the hard-power arsenal are, like soft-power weapons, used to get our husbands to do our will. With both approaches, the aim is manipulation. But husbands (and all of us) respond more favorably to respectful and honest interaction than to manipulation. The way we phrase things is critical, but it shouldn't come at the expense of the truth or with verbal weapons.

Sometimes in the pressures of daily life, husbands may speak using harsh words that feel like sword thrusts. This can be devastating, especially if what they say seems unwarranted and undeserved. Their words may push our anger buttons. At that point a woman may descend with wrath upon her husband like an elevator with a snapped cable.

These verbal sword fights never end well, do they? The house becomes filled with stress and tension, our peace is gone, and our relationship is cool and distant. Even our prayer time is affected. At best, this kind of hurtful interaction takes hours to overcome; at worst, days or weeks or even months. In fact, we have one friend whose anger button set off a ten-year cold war in her marriage. And, tragically, it's still going on.

One definition of *insanity* is doing the same things we've always done, yet expecting different results. We share that because there comes a point (and it's our prayer that it might be *today* for you) where we must decide there will be no more verbal sword-play. We resolve, *I'm going to be the voice of conciliation that puts God's principles ahead of my own agenda and feelings.*

Stop going in a direction you know will lead to unkind words. Stop arguing. Stop battling. Don't trade insult for insult, and don't tear down your husband. Be the light when darkness starts to gather. To quote a current media sage, it's time to "step up and be the hero."

One aspect of wisdom is recognizing that although your husband may not express his concerns with the kind of words you so long to hear, sometimes (maybe even often) he has a valid point. Some of us do spend too much money. Or talk on the phone too much. Or do whatever it is he's objecting to. Some-times wisdom means we simply admit to him that *he's right.* This action builds humility in us and does wonders for our men.

Over the years my sister Christine has been such an example to me in this business of marriage. Once, for instance, she was in the beginning stage of an argument with her husband, and it was about to escalate. He'd just raised his voice and accusingly blurted out, "You don't respect me!" She was about to respond with some cutting remark like, "Respect has to be earned, and you haven't earned it!"

But Christine had been praying about becoming a better wife, and something made her change what was about to come out of her mouth. Here's what she said instead: "I *do* respect you.

There are lots of things I admire and respect about you. I say good things about you to everyone. I absolutely *do* respect you."

Carl looked at her in stunned silence. She had tears of sincerity in her eyes. The quarrel was over. She'd stepped up to the plate.

Won't you step up as well?

BOTTOM LINE

The right words taste so much better
on our tongues than venom does.

30

Cut to the Chase

ONE OF THE BEST THINGS I (Nancy) have ever learned from Ray is the profitability of brevity in conversing. In the past, when I started to talk, Ray would ask (from experience), "Is this a long story?" Well, yes, it was going to be—and that wasn't the answer or the kind of story Ray wanted! At first I was hurt that my husband didn't want to hear all the details. But I had also noticed occasions when our sons would just leave the room as I rambled on, even though my daughters were very interested in what I had to say. Clearly, I needed to adapt myself to my husband's ways—and in that way please him.

You may be bristling at this. You may again be thinking, *Why do I have to adapt? Let him adapt to me!* But that's not God's directive, nor is it the way to glorify Him in your marriage.

Because Ray dislikes nearly all of my expansive details, I became a bullet-pointer. I can sum up *anything*! I can make an entire story one minute long—and Ray loves that. (So do my sons.)

And while I was learning to do this, the oddest thing happened to me. Now when I'm listening to others, I want them to be brief as well.

Studies show that men listen to about two sentences of what's being said before letting their minds go elsewhere—unless the topic is something they're personally interested in. So do a little research of your own. Ask your husband if you talk too much—and promise him you won't get angry if he says yes. If he does say you talk too much, make it your goal to shorten your chatter. Most men want to listen to their wives; they just want to know there'll be an out for them at some point.

BOTTOM LINE

Often when a woman talks less,
her husband will listen more.

31

You're Entitled!

WHEN YOU WRITE A BOOK, you're constantly bantering over titles. Not just for the book itself, but also for parts and chapters. The struggle is never ending.

Our first book went through six title changes before we arrived at *Is There a Moose in Your Marriage?* Even then, it was repackaged a few years later with yet a different title: *The Politically Incorrect Wife.*

Titles are everywhere. Almost every time you're introduced to someone, a title is attached to further explain your identity. You are *Jack's wife* or *Ryan's mother* or *Christine's sister* or *Thelma's daughter* or *John's boss.* Or the person introducing you might go with a career title: You're *a teacher* or *a nurse* or *a homemaker.* Or, simply, *my neighbor.* Or one of our favorites: *my friend.*

Just last week, my husband sent me this e-mail:

I love you, Connie!

Wes, Husband, Father, EMR Developer, Retired Golfer

You can see that titles were on Wes's mind that day.

Of course, this short, unexpected note meant everything to me. I've saved it, and I go back and read it almost every day.

On days I'm feeling blue and simply need to hear an "I love you" from Wes, I'll sometimes say, "Are you going to tell me you love me today, or do I need to go back and read that note in my inbox?" Wes understands instantly that I am playfully asking him to tell me I am loved.

Someone else had titles on His mind a long time ago. God! He has a title for you as a married woman. That title is significant, because it's His best for you as a wife. It's also significant because He knows your husband better than anyone else, because He created that man. God knows your husband's hopes and dreams, his insecurities and fears. He knows what wakes him up in the middle of the night, and He knows what causes him to sigh deeply. He knows his struggles. He knows his heart.

Don't you want to know those things about your husband as well? Maybe at times you no longer care, but you want to start caring again. God will help you. As you begin listening to God, *you* begin changing. It's the most miraculous, mysterious thing!

The bottom line is this: if you want your husband to listen to you, you need to start listening to God. That may be the most important statement in this book.

A godly woman is difficult to resist. She has something about her that's unlike any other woman alive—and this difference is alluring to a husband. We've heard hundreds of stories from women who decided to model themselves after God's plan for their lives—to embrace the title He ordained for them—and this is the kindling that caused a cold marriage to become warm again. In fact, it was the very thing that began the transformations in our own marriages, so the subject is dear to our hearts.

God revealed His title for wives as He put the finishing touches on His creation. Our title is so simple and direct that it will take your breath away. Listen again to *His* words regarding wives: "It is not good (sufficient, satisfactory) that the man should be alone; I will make him a *helper* meet (suitable, adapted, complementary) for him" (Genesis 2:18, AMP). There it is, God's perfect plan for a wife. She is to be a helper to her husband.

We can almost hear the gasps from some of you as you read this. We gasped ourselves. I (Connie) even went digging through other resources to find another word I liked better. But there was no other word. No matter which Scripture translation or interpretation I checked, the same word was used: *helper.*

I wasn't impressed or encouraged by that fact one bit. I'd practically stood on my head in the early years trying to help Wes, and it seemed to me that he hardly noticed. I didn't do this because I was trying to embrace God's plan for my life. At that point I didn't even know God's plan for my life, but I did want to please Wes.

However, as I mentioned earlier, I grew tired of doing all the work, and I placed efforts on hold until his efforts caught up. Then, fifteen years into the marriage, I heard—for the first time ever—a wife called by the title "helper."

I can tell you the hairs on my neck stood out farther than they ever had. After all, I was far too much on the ball to be anyone's helper—except maybe to my kids! Helping my children was, of course, a noble cause. Helping my husband, on the other hand, was not.

But then I learned that helper is a title God bestowed upon Himself (see Isaiah 41:10). So I, Mrs. High and Mighty, was forced to consider this important question: if helper is a good enough title for God, shouldn't it be good enough for me?

My (Nancy's) story is a bit different. I'd been married for over twenty years when I realized God had a plan for my life. My own plan wasn't working well, and I'd recently committed my life to Him. So I decided to see what He had to say about marriage, an area where I'd struggled for so long.

Over the years, I'd developed this little hobby called anger. It surprised me that I'd done this, because I'm not an angry person. But marriage seemed to bring it out in me, and some days I spent more time being angry than not. If Ray hurt my feelings or didn't do what I thought he should, my little hobby came roaring to life. I was weary of living like this, and I'm sure Ray and the children were as well—walking on eggshells is never fun. Then I decided to do things God's way.

I completely agreed that Ray *needed* a helper—that much

was obvious. I just didn't feel Ray deserved such help from me. But I was determined to do things God's way, so I began.

My behavior began to change drastically. I began treating Ray with respect instead of indifference. I stopped nagging and nitpicking. I began taking him a cup of coffee every morning as a way of expressing my love. I would have never done that before. I felt like a different woman, and home became a warmer place, a safer place.

As I exchanged my ways for God's ways, I began falling in love with Ray all over again. I felt a deeper love for him than I ever had. This continues to leave me speechless today. I know that the change began when I learned Ray needed a helper...and when I realized that *I* needed help even more. What a comfort it was to discover I had a helper! My helper was God, and He so wants to be your helper too.

Thus began the changes in our own marriages. Embracing our title of helper was the first step. Our lives have never been the same since.

Do we still struggle? Yes.

Do arguments still occur? Yes—sometimes daily. (Sometimes more often than that!)

But we don't struggle as hard or for as long, because we want to please God. Neither do we hold against our husbands so many qualities that are just unique to men.

For years, we tried to make our husbands see and do things our way. We tried to mold them into our mentality. How ridiculous! No one expects a dog to meow like a cat, but for some odd reason, we expected our husbands to respond as women would.

Our first book, *The Politically Incorrect Wife,* is all about your role as a wife, so if you're curious for more, you might consider reading it. For now, we just want to plant this small seed: God has a plan for your life. As part of that plan, God has a title for you as a married woman, and that title is helper.

If you want to find true joy and satisfaction in your life, there's only one route to take, and the journey requires you to use God's road map, not your own. It's that simple…and it's that hard.

Every woman we speak to longs for joy, peace, love, and satisfaction, all of which can seem so elusive. As you begin living by God's principles, He'll begin to fill your heart to overflowing with these things. But they won't be found apart from Him. You can have all the wealth, all the prestige, all the trappings this world has to offer, but you won't find joy and contentment apart from God.

On Christmas Day in 1970, I (Connie) remember thinking Daddy and Mom must have had a hard year, because there were so few gifts for us to open that morning. It didn't matter to us girls, though. We loved Christmas regardless of the quantity of presents.

As the morning was winding down and we were picking up the tissue paper and wrappings, Daddy said, "Wait a minute! I think I see one more gift hiding in the tree." Our eyes immediately scanned the tree, and sure enough, a small box tucked into the branches had gone unnoticed until now.

We couldn't imagine what was going on, because Santa Claus normally didn't operate in this manner. Yes, we still celebrated Santa, because my six-year-old sister Anita was completely besotted by him. The rest of us girls were beyond that. My older sister had her driver's license already, and the next younger sister and I would be getting our licenses shortly.

We quickly unwrapped the box, and inside was a note: *The rest of your Christmas gift is in the barn.* We gleefully headed out the door with our parents close behind us. We reached the barn, but it was locked. Daddy reached into his pocket for the key, unlocked the door, and slid it open. There before us was a shiny Oldsmobile, used but just gleaming. Its grill and headlights sparkled in the light. It was several years old, but Daddy had shined it to look brand-new.

We stood for a moment just gazing at it. Each of us girls knew it had come at great cost for our parents, because there was never a lot of money to spare when we were growing up. This fact made us appreciate the gift even more.

Yet, as excited as each of us was, do you know who was the most excited of all? My dad. He himself had chosen that gift for us, and he'd worked on it until it was spotless, driven it home in the middle of the night, backed it into the barn, and then placed that small box in the tree to await our discovering it.

As excited as my dad was that day, you have a heavenly Father with a storehouse of far more wonderful gifts He has chosen with you in mind. He's waiting to throw open the door to you and shower you with everything He has to offer…but the one requirement is that you choose to live His way.

Today, right now, even as you're reading this, won't you consider committing yourself to living by His principles? If so, know that a great way to start is to accept the high and holy calling of being a helper to your husband.

BOTTOM LINE

*Men need help, and your man needs
your help. Does he have it?*

32

HE'S YOUR DEFENDER... AND YOU'RE HIS

WE HAVE A SIMPLE QUESTION for you. It's one of the questions that helped spark the changes in our own marriages. It's also the question that, once we acknowledged it, began the journey to Wes and Ray wanting to listen to us again.

Here's the question: is your husband lonely? If he is, did you realize you're called to do something about it?

For a long time, we didn't realize we are called to do something about our husbands' loneliness. We'd both been married for years before we understood that our husbands' aloneness was part of the reason we were created. Isn't that amazing? Although a man is meant to defend his wife, she, in turn, is meant to defend him—against aloneness. That truth dates back to the garden.

On every day of the week of Creation, when God created something, He stepped back and said, "This is good." But when He stepped back and saw that Adam was alone, He said, "It is not good." (See Genesis 1–2.)

Reflect on that again. We have a perfect God, who created a perfect world. He Himself is the Artist, and every stroke is by His hand. Yet the Artist Himself noted that something was missing. Some*one* was missing.

Woman—and all that she brings to the life of man—was missing from his life. God took note of this, then He created Eve. She completed not only Adam, but Creation itself. In a sense, Eve was God's exclamation point to everything He'd made. Some women say today that God is anti-woman. Nothing could be further from the truth.

Adam could name the animals and tend them. He could work the soil and produce food to be eaten. He had plenty to do, and he surely didn't have much to complain about. Yet he was lonely. Nothing in God's creation satisfied his soul like Eve did.

The same is true today. Nothing in your husband's world can satisfy his longing to be admired and accepted like you can. He has a deep need—a primal need—to know that he matters greatly to you and that you respect him as a man. Does he know that? Or might he secretly feel that you think life would barely miss a beat—even that you'd be better off—if something happened to him?

If your husband is lonely, this goes directly against God's

plan for his life—and yours. We understand you may be lonely too. We were. But once we came face to face with God's spoken word regarding our husbands' loneliness, our own didn't seem so important. And as we began to defend our husbands against the enemy of being lonely, our own loneliness seemed to disappear as well.

There's something mysterious about how everything changes when you set into motion God's plan for your life. You start out thinking, *Well, he doesn't deserve this. He's so self-centered and doesn't seem to care at all about my needs.* Then, as you step out in faith and begin to reinvest in his life, your changed behavior becomes the impetus for changed behavior in your husband. More often than not, your efforts will prove life changing for both of you.

But *even if your husband doesn't change,* you reap the reward that comes from doing the right thing. You might experience a tremendous sense of peace. Perhaps you'll sleep better at night. Or you may find you're more patient in general and, as a result, your kids' behavior begins to change as well. You might find yourself thinking far less about how your husband drives you crazy and far more about how thankful you are he's in your life. It's unexplainable.

Regardless of how your husband responds to your efforts, we know one thing: a change will occur in you. Why? Because God rewards hearts that are yielded to Him. Again, it's that simple...and that hard. On those days when you find it difficult to stay on this course, take comfort in remembering that God will never call you to do anything He won't equip you to do.

Listen again: "It is not good for the man to be alone." God is speaking. The King of kings…the Lord of lords…the God of gods…*is speaking.* So the real question is, are you listening?

If you want your life to change, if you want your marriage to change, the wisest thing you can ever do is listen to God when He speaks and then obey Him. You don't have to understand the reason for His commands or even agree with Him, but if you want change in your life, start listening to the One who can bring change in ways you never dreamed of.

Lonely men aren't good listeners—at least, not to their wives.

BOTTOM LINE

If God's answer to Adam's aloneness was Eve, then His answer to your husband's aloneness is_____ .

PART 4

AHA! MOMENTS

33

GUESS WHO GAVE HIM HIS PERSONALITY?

IN THEIR OUTSTANDING BOOK *The Two Sides of Love,* Gary Smalley and John Trent brilliantly use four members of the animal kingdom to define human personalities:

- The Lion loves to take charge and is bold, assertive, competitive, and purposeful. His or her motto is, "Let's do it now!"
- The Beaver is deliberate, detailed, orderly, factual, scheduled, and controlled. The beaver's motto is, "How was it done in the past?"
- The Otter is a visionary, fun-loving, energetic motivator who is almost always optimistic. An otter's motto is, "Trust me! It'll work out!"

- The Golden Retriever is loyal and undemanding, avoids conflict, dislikes change, and is sympathetic. The motto here is, "Let's keep things the way they are."

Where do you see yourself in this list? And where do you see your husband?

My sister and I (Nancy) have developed a theory that male lions hunt female otters more often than otters seek out lions. Apparently lions find otters to be worth their weight in gold and absolutely delightful to be around. So they pursue otters—until they get them to the altar. Once married, the lion begins a quiet and pensive study of the otter and sometimes wishes his otter were a bit more lionlike than otterlike.

Christine and I are otters. Our husbands, Carl and Ray, are lions. At first, before we realized that many others on this planet aren't otters, these two men puzzled us greatly.

When I visited Carl and Christine last month, I noted the unspoken-unless-violated rules Carl had nailed invisibly to the wall. The door to the powder room, for instance, was to be left completely open. If you got ice water from the fridge, you had to re-press the button so only ice would come out next time. The air conditioner was to remain set at seventy-four degrees. Anything you used was to be returned to its original place. These rules are based on Carl's logic, and they were all carefully formulated (I'm sure) to make the household run smoothly and neatly.

There's also apparently an exactly correct spot in the garage for Christine to park the car. (Carl likes to have plenty of room to walk in front of the cars.) So Carl offers helpful suggestions like, "The handle of your front door should be even with mine. It's not that hard."

Often, when she and I would come home after being out together, Christine would get back into the car and tweak it an inch or two. Or Carl, after helping us in with our packages, would return to tweak the car himself.

This is puzzling to both of us. We're thinking, *Why does this matter? What difference could a few inches make?*

Now Carl is a wonderful man, and there's absolutely nothing wrong with his asking for adherence to a few things that are important to him. And I'm guessing that your husband also has certain things he likes done in a certain way. Some of the items may puzzle you, but our hope is that you'll not let this typically guy thing be a matter of contention in your marriage. After all, we wives have our own issues, which we're sure guys find as perplexing to them as theirs are to us.

What we women sometimes do, however, is make an issue over a simple request. We think or even say, "Why in the world would something so small matter so much to you?" By asking that question, we've actually answered it as well: that "something so small" isn't hard to do. So why not just follow the few house rules your husband has come up with?

Carl adores Christine. When I'm there, he hugs her all the time, zips by and playfully kisses her, and always makes sure she's taken care of. Christine's gracious acceptance of his house rules reveals the love she has for Carl. He's her knight in shining armor, and she shows her respect for him by following the few rules he has requested.

And it's no surprise, I might add, that Carl finds Christine incredibly interesting to listen to.

BOTTOM LINE

Don't let small things become big issues.

34

Maybe I'm Not as Right as I Thought I Was

ONE OF THE BIGGEST MISTAKES a woman makes when communicating with her husband is to determine she's right about a certain topic regardless of what her husband says. This is especially true if the topic involves intangibles such as attitudes, feelings, and motives. She may insist she's right, but she probably has a husband who has completely tuned her out... and who can blame him?

Unless your husband is a chronic liar or a sociopath, why would you assume you know your husband's thoughts and feelings better than he does? If you want your husband to listen to you, begin listening to him and accepting what he says without thinking your opinion overrides his.

As we mature in our faith and grow in wisdom, those of us with this "I'm right and you're wrong" mind-set will hopefully experience the humbling epiphany of an "aha!" moment in this regard: sometimes *we* are wrong in our perception of things. A friend of ours experienced this kind of moment. She held onto her trump card for over a year before she finally understood why her husband had responded as he did in a certain situation. Here's the story of her "aha!" moment.

Eric and Stacey are friends of ours. An attorney, Eric is highly competitive, and he loves a challenge. Stacey is easygoing, enjoys people, and loves to have fun. She can have fun, win or lose, while Eric has never associated losing with fun.

One Friday afternoon Eric called Stacey to see if they had any plans for the evening. They discussed what they could do. Knowing Eric loves to golf and that his week had been especially difficult, Stacey suggested they meet at the golf course. He could play golf while she rode in the cart. (She wasn't a golfer, but she enjoyed watching him.) Eric thought her suggestion bordered on brilliant, and he readily agreed. A few hours later, they were on the golf course and Eric was teeing off.

It soon became evident his game was off. He bogeyed his way through the first couple holes, and he couldn't seem to buy a putt no matter what.

Stacey sat in the cart and cheered him on. She felt bad that he wasn't playing well, but she was still having a wonderful time. The evening was beautiful, the sun was warm across her back, and she was looking forward to going out to dinner once they finished the nine holes.

However, the evening took a sharp turn on the seventh hole. It was as if the golf ball developed a mind of its own. Each time Eric attempted to putt, the ball would roll past the hole. He'd walk over to the ball and putt again, only to see it slide past the hole in the opposite direction. This happened time and again.

It reminded Stacey of a game she used to play as a young girl called Annie Annie Over. So after the fourth missed putt, she called out in a cheerful, lilting voice, "Are we having fun yet?"

Her remark was intended to encourage him, but it did just the opposite. Eric looked at her in disbelief, picked up his ball, marched to the cart, and drove back to the clubhouse.

"What are we doing?" Stacey asked.

"Going home," Eric replied tersely. "I'm through golfing for today."

Stacey was speechless. What on earth was wrong with him? "What are you talking about? It's a beautiful evening. I don't understand."

Eric kept driving to the clubhouse. He was obviously irritated, but Stacey couldn't imagine why. She revisited every hole in her mind. She had cheered him on at each one, even at the Annie Annie Over hole. Plus, she'd remained upbeat and jovial, even with his constant complaining about his poor play.

"Did I say something wrong?" she asked, certain that she hadn't but hoping to get a clue into what was going on.

Eric turned and scowled at her, "I can't believe you said, 'Are we having fun yet?' on that last hole. Obviously, I wasn't golfing well, and I wasn't having fun at all. You take the fun out of everything I do."

Stacey was speechless. Flabbergasted. She'd given him nonstop applause on every hole. Besides that, she was the one who had initiated this golf outing so he could relax and unwind—which obviously hadn't happened. Furthermore, there were plenty of other things she would have preferred doing besides golfing, but she had been thinking of him. And now he had the nerve to ask why she couldn't be more supportive? Unbelievable!

However, the night was still young, and she certainly didn't want to spend the weekend like this, so she decided to salvage what she could of the evening and the ensuing weekend. It didn't matter who was right or wrong. Obviously he'd misunderstood what she was trying to do on the last hole, so she attempted to explain that her remark was actually meant to be encouraging and that she was really just trying to lighten the mood since he seemed so disgruntled.

"I wasn't disgruntled," he said in exasperation. "And I'm so tired of you telling me how I feel." Then he said the words that put her over the edge: "Let's be honest. There's no way you were trying to encourage me by saying what you did. Who are you trying to kid?"

At this point Stacey decided to forget about salvaging the rest of the weekend. Now she was mad. Absolutely furious. She was as mad as she could ever remember being in her marriage, and maybe in her entire life. She had been unjustly accused—completely and totally unjustly.

By this time, they'd returned the cart and were in the parking lot. He threw his clubs in the trunk, and she threw herself in the car. They drove home in silence, the air thick with tension and anger. When they got home, she sat in the car until he'd gone inside. Then she took a walk around the block. She had no desire to be around him.

When she returned home, he'd gone to a movie. That was perfectly fine with her.

When he got home from the movie, she was already in bed, pretending to be asleep, which was perfectly fine with him. He slipped into bed, staying on the far edge of his side of the mattress, while she tossed and turned on the far edge of hers.

Morning came, and the awkwardness continued. Finally, Eric brought up the night before and tried to explain to Stacey why he felt as he did and why her remark was discouraging to him. She, however, was in no mood to listen to anything other than an outright apology. Clearly he was the one at fault, and she wasn't going to budge an inch until she heard him admit that he'd behaved outrageously.

Have you found yourself in a similar situation...over something trivial in nature, with the seeds of a misunderstanding not only sown but watered and spread with fertilizer?

Let's assume, for a moment, that you reacted as Stacey did.

Let's also assume that you believe you were completely right—about everything. Now stop and ponder this for a moment: how high a price are you willing to pay to be right?

- a strained relationship with your husband?
- a lost weekend?
- a lost night of sleep?
- a lost marriage?

Is the cost of being right really worth it? Furthermore, who's to say you're right? Chances are, your husband feels he's just as right as you.

Sometimes being right comes at a very high price. The cost can take a toll on your marriage for years, especially if you're someone who nearly always thinks she's right, as many of us do.

Read the rest of Stacey and Eric's story.

Just over a year later, they were out to dinner with another couple. Like Eric, this man was intense, highly competitive, and an avid golfer. He asked Eric if Stacey ever golfed with him. Eric didn't quite know what to say, so Stacey gave a brief summary of how they once did, and why they stopped.

When Stacey got to the Annie Annie Over hole and described how she'd called out, "Are we having fun yet?" to encourage Eric, the man stopped her in her tracks.

"Are you kidding me?" he asked. "Do you really think I'm going to believe you were trying to encourage him with that remark? You don't ever say something like that to a guy who's already frustrated at how he's golfing, let alone say it on a hole like that. You're lucky he didn't wrap his golf club around your neck."

His response wasn't at all what Stacey expected. She thought everyone who heard the story would surely agree with her. After all, she was right!

She attempted to defend her case to this obviously clueless man, but he would have none of it. "Say what you want about how hurt you felt," he said, "but I'm siding with Eric. By now you should know a remark like that—especially on the golf course when he's already playing really badly—takes the wind right out of a man's sails. Good grief, how long have you two been married? Twenty years, right? You should know him better than that by now."

For the first time in over a year, Stacey considered Eric's position. Yes, he'd misunderstood what she really was trying to do, but she'd refused to listen to him when he tried to explain how he felt. Suddenly, that seemed just as bad.

To top it off, she had seethed over the whole incident from time to time for an entire year. What a waste! She also remembered how she'd treated Eric when she was secretly seething, and the memories made her grimace with regret.

Hearing the other man's perspective—which she knew mirrored what Eric had tried to tell her the morning after the incident—caused her to see things afresh:

- She wasn't always right.
- She doesn't always have to be right.

- Sometimes a husband and wife just disagree on how they see things.
- Sometimes doing the right thing means simply letting go of anger.
- In the midst of conflict, it's wise to listen more than you talk.
- Sometimes guys get really upset over what we gals would consider stupid stuff. That's just the way it is…and that's okay.

Dinner with that couple was a watershed moment for Stacey. We hope this chapter will serve the same purpose for you as well.

BOTTOM LINE

As women we tend to think we're misunderstood in the marriage relationship. But at times we're the ones who misunderstand.

35

THE NEXT TIME

As I (Connie) write this chapter, it's almost eleven in the morning, and I'm sitting at my desk with my robe on. This is a rarity. Normally I'm up by five, dressed, and ready to go. I can't remember sitting around in my robe like this since Christmas Day almost a year ago. I must admit, though, it feels good, especially because I know it will probably be a long while before I do it again.

I'm in my robe because I forgot to lay out my clothes last night so I could put them on this morning without waking up Wes, who's just returned from being out of town. So I felt for my robe, found it, and—lo and behold—I'm still in it! The day is gray and cold outside, and I have this sense I'm playing hooky from school as I sit here and type. But it does feel good.

A couple of times I've gotten up and flipped on the television for a brief distraction. One program dealt with the issue of why certain women are drawn to married men. The person speaking gave four possibilities as to why this occurs:

1. *Comparison.* Have you ever noticed that when you're at a restaurant, the food on someone else's plate often looks better than what you ordered? According to the experts, this is the same kind of mentality that causes women to go after married men. They want what someone else has.

2. *Family pattern.* If a woman came from a home in which there was marital straying, she'll often repeat the same behavior in her own life.

3. *Low self-esteem.* Enough said.

4. *Competition.* This kind of woman gets a great deal of satisfaction knowing she can win a man away from his wife (although the expert being interviewed went on to explain that most men don't end up leaving their wives for such women).

We hope you aren't in a situation anywhere close to this. But the topic has prompted us to write about something to help keep your marriage warm and inviting, and therefore help you guard against the advances of others who may be looking to make inroads into your marriage. We call it "the next time" ministry.

There was a time in both of our marriages when we found ourselves more often than not irritated with our husbands. We didn't know each other then, but our stories are quite similar. Over time we each developed the habit of treating our husbands in a way that might be described as passive-aggressive. (To put it bluntly, we treated them coldly if they didn't make us happy.)

At some point this little habit became a way of life. Marriage wasn't pleasant for our husbands or for us, but neither of us realized we had the power to do anything else. After all, we were women. We had feelings—a whole lot of them, in fact. And isn't that what women do—live by their feelings?

Well, it might be that way, but it shouldn't be. To live by your feelings is to forfeit your power to be positive and to accomplish good and worthwhile things. You begin to empower the wrong, negative part of yourself. So what's the way out?

First we need to remember that feelings follow actions. So if you want to feel differently, act differently. You see, you can choose to act in a loving manner whether you *feel* like it or not. Doing this makes life so much easier—especially in regard to marriage. You'll find you're less prone to anger, and you'll have a new freedom that's refreshing and energizing. Being irritated all the time just flat wears you out, and it makes you unpleasant to be around.

One day a while ago, I (Connie) found myself slipping back into this live-by-feelings pattern. Thankfully, my twin daughters were home from college for the summer, and they said, "Mom, what's up? You're irritated with Dad all the time."

I wanted to say, "And rightfully so," but I knew in my heart that I was the one who needed to change. Plus I wanted our daughters to always hold Wes in the highest regard. But I needed help. I felt as if someone pulled the plug on my desire to be a good wife, and I was headed down the drain fast.

To get back into the swing of things, I determined to treat Wes respectfully and lovingly the very next time I saw him. That's all, simply *the next time*. I didn't commit to the next ten years, but just the very next time. I could do that. And I did.

Then, after that, I'd make the same decision: to treat him respectfully the very next time we were together. And I did.

Slowly, decision by decision, I got out of the mud hole I'd fallen into. I could do something once. Then I could do it again. After all, life really is comprised of a series of decisions we each make one at a time.

Experts tell us it takes approximately twenty-one days for a habit to form. So whatever you need to be doing in your marriage, start doing it today, and continue doing it—the next time—for twenty more days. And see what happens.

This "next time" principle hasn't been scientifically tested, but it helps me stay on track even as I sit here in my robe and write. You see, Wes came home unexpectedly just a few minutes ago. He'd forgotten something and swung by to pick it up. Since this whole "next time" subject was on my mind, I jumped up, ran out the front door when I saw him pull in, and gave him a big hug. He folded me into his arms, and a big smile burst across his face. I think my response meant the world to him. Of course he didn't say, "Gee, Connie, your doing this means the world to me." But I could tell he was touched. This unexpected moment in our day set the tone for a wonderful Friday night.

What might happen if you decided to begin practicing this "next time" principle in your own marriage? It sure can't hurt, and we can positively guarantee you one thing: no matter what your husband does or doesn't do, you'll be changed.

Wes called me later during this same day and said, "I was just sitting here thinking how much your love and support mean to me. I really appreciate how you've always stood by me through the years." Yet a few summers before, back when I was struggling with my feelings and my daughters questioned me about my constant irritation with Wes, I could have answered them along these lines: "Well, you know what, too bad. That's how I feel. I'm just going to sit here and wait for your father to change before I do anything. I'm tired of always being the one to rally the troops." I would have set a poor example for my girls. I would also have opened wide the door for my heart—as well as Wes's—to have frozen over again.

Sometimes women take on more of the relationship burden than guys do. As we've said before, women generally are more relational. Remember, God created Adam and told him to work the ground. Today, men still gather and talk about work and sports. They're creatures who *do*. Eve, however, was created especially for relationship. Adam was lonely, and he needed a companion, a helper. Eve was God's answer to this.

Women long for relationship—especially with our husbands. When we gather, we talk about our husbands and children, about relationship issues…about our hopes and dreams…about our hearts. We speak of many other things, such as work and sports, but relationship issues still top the list.

These different focuses simply reflect our created function, our inherent wiring, which recent scientific discoveries such as brain mapping have given further credence to. As a male friend said to us not long ago, "You know, ladies, men really aren't that difficult to understand. Our needs are very few. We want you to treat us well. We want to come home to peace. We want our physical needs met. Pretty much, that's it." We've run this comment by dozens of men in the past few weeks, and all have agreed with our friend.

There was one more thing that many of them added to the list. Can you guess what it was? It probably comes as no surprise that it wasn't "to talk more" or "to bond more" or "to go for more walks." Their addition was this: "We want something to eat when we're hungry."

Guys want their physical needs met. And that includes sex.

Because guys are wired to be so physical, sex is a huge part of the marriage relationship for them. When guys complain about their sexual needs not being met, the number one reason for the grumbling is…their sexual needs *aren't* being met.

We, as woman, want to "make love," an activity that involves the all-important (to us) feeling of emotional validation and connection. It helps us to remember that to a guy, physical intimacy (what he wants) leads to emotional intimacy (what we want), while for women, emotional intimacy leads to physical intimacy. We are simply created differently in this regard. Neither is wrong. Just different.

So in a marriage, if one person would take the first step and attempt to meet the other's needs, this effort would go a long way in helping the relationship. Hopefully, your husband is making an effort to meet your emotional needs even though they're a foreign language to him. But if and when he forgets to do this, it doesn't make him the enemy. He's not wrong or shallow because his sexual responses trigger differently than yours do. He's not you. You aren't him. God created both of you—and He created you extremely differently. Your innate differences were His idea.

We invite you to consider the following possibility: your strengths (including your relational giftedness) plus your husband's strengths (including his task-related giftedness) equals one whole, balanced person. You really do complete each other.

So it's definitely time for us women to get over ourselves and stop being mad at our husbands for being men. It's time we stopped trying to turn them into male versions of ourselves.

It takes two to make a marriage…really, three, including the Lord. It takes just one to break it. It takes just one to make it miserable. And it takes just one to begin to turn it around in love.

Are you willing to be that one?

BOTTOM LINE

*You, too, have a helper. He's the One
who wants to make your marriage
not only happy but sacred.*

36

Uncovering How Men Communicate

Every Tuesday for the past five years, Connie and I have left our homes before dawn and gone to the KGBI radio station where we do a segment called *Lifewalk*. Roger Manning, one of the hosts, is an uncommonly gracious and funny man. So we asked him to give us a man's point of view regarding the listening factors in a man's life. We know you'll be extremely enlightened as you read what he has to say.

A Man's Point of View

The truth is, we men put what our wives want to talk about into four categories. (We didn't make these categories up. They're in the "Guy Handbook" somewhere. I'd tell you where, but I seem to have lost my copy. Anyway, I know what it says. All guys do.)

Most of these categories probably offer the opportunity for discussion, and in just a minute I'll get to how I think wives can make that happen. First, let me define the categories.

Category One: She Cares

Here's a shocker for you: men and women are made differently. Therefore some things that women feel are important enough to discuss don't strike guys in the same way. (How's that for diplomacy?) The color of the petunias in the front flower bed might just fall into that category. Likewise, there are things guys think should be discussed that women don't see the need for, like the importance in football of having two down blockers on the weak side if an option play is to be successful. But we don't bother our wives with these kinds of topics, so we don't need a "He Cares" category.

Category Two: We Care

Just because guys can be kind of sloppy, single minded, and even a bit buffoonish at times doesn't mean we don't care about some things and want to talk about them. Of course we want to talk about our shared responsibilities, desires, and dreams for the future. We should also want to talk about God and our daily walk with Him.

I'll bare my soul here and offer a moment of unvarnished truth. (But if you tell any of the brothers I told you this, I will deny it to my dying day.) There are lots of things in this category a woman would never even imagine. For some of these things, we need other guys to talk with. And for a great number of them, we should (and need to) listen to our wives. In just a minute I'll explain those and how to go about engaging your husband in conversations about them.

Category Three: Everybody Cares

Here you go, ladies. There are some things—a tornado in the neighborhood, a burst water pipe in the basement, the dog getting hit by a car—that a guy will listen to no matter the time or circumstances. There are three basic conditions here:

1. The subject is cataclysmic in nature (especially if it touches someone in the family).
2. The situation needs a solution right now to avoid further damage.
3. The situation will affect his family, finances, love life, or stomach.

If the topic meets one of these criteria, you go right ahead and start talking, anytime, anywhere. A guy will listen even if he doesn't want to.

Category Four: Who Cares?

Now, this isn't meant to be mean. But it's a fact of life: there are some things no one in this world wants to talk about. On occasion, men actually bring up some of them. Usually, however, they're doing it to joke, which is entertainment and therefore exempt from the "Who Cares?" category. But sometimes men are just off base, not thinking, or trying to impress someone. But I digress… To a guy's way of thinking, topics in this fourth category don't need to be talked about anytime by anybody.

Now to the meat of the matter. Let me go through these categories one by one and see if I can shed some light on the best way to get your man to listen to you on a topic from each of them.

Revisiting Category One: She Cares

I have to admit, this is one of the tougher categories when it comes to getting a subject off the table and into committee. You have to be creative and maybe even a little coercive. These topics are interesting to you and not at all interesting to your husband, so he's not predisposed to listen simply because of the topic. Here you have to rely on what I call the Three Ts of Talking: *timing, tact, tantalizing.*

Timing is always important, but never more than when you know your guy isn't really going to be interested in what you have to say. So you have to choose a time when he doesn't have anything more important on his mind. Now I know I just left myself and all the guys open on that one. You'll likely say he rarely has *anything* important on his mind, just football, or mowing the lawn, or cutting his toenails. But remember, we're talking in relation to what *you* want to talk about. All those things are steps above whether we should plant red or purple petunias.

I took a break from writing just a moment ago and went

upstairs where my wife is painting the dining room for the second time in two months (Don't ask me why. That's another book.) I was kind of wandering around aimlessly, checking the refrigerator twice for a snack...

Stop! Right there! That's it. When your guy is wandering and stands with the refrigerator open for the second time in just minutes, you have him. That's when he's most vulnerable to conversations. If he can look in a refrigerator and not choose anything, he really doesn't have anything on his mind. Obviously he's not hungry because he didn't choose anything. There are no ball games or good war movies on in the fridge. He's loose, without purpose, plan, or direction.

So Jodie asked if I was hungry, and I said, "Not really." (This isn't actually true, because a guy can always eat if he sees something he likes.) She came over, put her arm around my neck, and explained that she's finishing this coat of paint and then she's going to grill steaks. She already had potatoes in the oven. We stood there embracing for a moment before she said she'd decided to paint the dining area the same color as the darker trim in the living room. Before I knew it, I was giving my opinion of that idea, and of the color itself, and of the living room in general, and—well, I was listening to her talk about a subject in which I couldn't have been the least bit interested.

You see, Jodie had picked the perfect *time*. I was doing nothing, and I had nothing in particular on my mind. Her *tact* was apparent in her decision not to initiate that specific subject by title, which would have sent me running. She simply explained what was going on as part of her plan to fix me a *tantalizing* steak dinner.

There you have the Three Ts of Talking.

Revisiting Category Two: We Care

I love my wife more than anyone else on this earth. I believe she loves me more than anyone else on this earth—except Tom Selleck (just a little inside joke). Together, we love God more than anything on this earth or in the heavens. So, we have a lot of things we really care about together. These things should be the easiest for her to get me to listen to, and for the most part, they are. However, just because these topics are what I *should* listen to is no guarantee I will.

The real key to getting me to listen here is to remind me of who I am. You see, I grew up being a boy. I guess that's not surprising; most guys do. What I mean is, I didn't grow up being prepared to be a man, much less a godly man. That wasn't the way things worked in my house.

Now, I try very hard to be what my friend Stu Weber calls a Four Pillar Man. That is, I try to be a fair and just King in my life, family, and church; I try to be a Tender Warrior who fearlessly protects by defending and (when necessary) attacking; I make every effort to be a wise Mentor while living according to God's instruction manual and teaching the path outlined there; and I want to always be a true and faithful Friend to everyone, but especially to my wife and family, and to my brothers and sisters in Christ.

See, the problem isn't only that I was brought up a boy and got a late start on this Four Pillar Man stuff, but I'm also a son of Adam. To borrow a line from a really great TV commercial, "I've fallen and I can't get up." At least not without some help. And right there in Genesis it says my wife was created as a helper suitable for me.

So, I have to rely on my wife to help me anytime I start demonstrating just how fallen I am. And she does. When my wife decides there's something in this category she wants to talk about and I need to listen, she just has to remind me who I am and that she's trying to help me.

Then I'm listening—humbly, energetically, lovingly.

Revisiting Category Three: Everybody Cares

The topics in this category are the easiest to get us talking about with you. You know your man's heart, or you wouldn't love him enough to be with him and you wouldn't be reading to find out how to get closer to him. Since you know your man's heart, you know what he cares most about. So I'm guessing you've never had him ignore you when you were trying to get him to listen to you about one of these topics.

When something is threatening the health, wealth, and happiness of your family, your guy wants to be the first to know. That's the way we're made. We're warriors, and we're ready to step into the fray to protect and defend what's ours. We don't need any mollycoddling. There's no need to be tactful. There's no need to bribe us.

This is an instance when you can call us on the phone at work. This is an instance when you can walk right in and turn the TV off even though there are just two minutes left in a tie ball game between Nebraska and Texas. This may not be the only place we'll listen to you, but it's the place we listen most attentively, especially if we can provide a solution for whatever situation is unfolding.

We're kings! We're warriors! We're problem solvers! We're men! Don't you dare not tell us!

Revisiting Category Four: Who Cares?

I'm sorry, but there's no way around this one. Believe me, I love Nancy and Connie like my own sisters, and I would gladly spill the beans if there were any way I could help here. But maybe knowing there's no way your husband will listen to "Who Cares?" topics is actually some help. Bottom line, you can avoid this category all together. At least you can save yourselves the "agony of defeat." (Don't you love sports analogies?)

When you ask a guy if he thinks it hurts a worm when you put it on the hook, he's just not going to be listening unless he's a youngster who has never heard a woman ask this before. Then he's only listening so he can go back, tell his buddies, and have a good laugh at your expense. And in that case, your guy won't be challenged about bringing up the subject because, as mentioned earlier, topics used for a joke and humor are exempted. Or your guy might bring up the topic in front of your mother or best friend to impress her with his sincerity and kind heart. This too was covered earlier and is exempt as well.

One more thing about this category. If you really think about it, you yourself probably weren't really interested in the topic; you were just trying to make conversation to get the big lug to pay some attention to you. Hey, that's okay. Just pick a topic he cares about, and you're on your way.

———

In closing, let me just say I'm relying on your discretion, ladies, to keep me out of trouble. I take great risk passing along age-old secrets, heretofore discernible only by an in-depth study of Leonardo da Vinci's paintings and cracking the code to my brother's gym locker. Should it become known that I've leaked any of this information to those of the fairer gender, I will, no doubt, be ostracized and set upon by ruffians at my every step outside the walls of my castle. God bless you.

BOTTOM LINE

Talk about things your husband cares about.

37

You Might Be Surprised

We're always surprised by how much we learn when we undertake the writing of a book. It's like teaching: the teacher learns far more than her students. To follow are some nuggets we learned (or relearned) as we researched this book. We thought they might be of interest to you.

- Most men think that once they're married, their wives understand and will remember that they're loved. For a guy, the deal is done. Finished. It's a matter that doesn't really need to be revisited over and over again. He's surprised that his wife sees this issue differently. She actually wants to hear "I love you" every single day—and sometimes more than once. Most men simply don't understand this. Your husband assumes you know he loves you until he tells you differently.

    Takeaway: He loves you.

- Women often use silence as a form of punishment if they're feeling irritated or angry at someone. This is an effective tactic when used on other women, but it doesn't work nearly so well on men. Most men *enjoy* silence, even if it's occurring because they've landed in the doghouse. They may be in the doghouse, but at least the doghouse is peaceful and quiet. The roof may cave in soon—as he well knows—but until it does, he'll enjoy his brief respite.

  Takeaway: Stop using the silent treatment.

- Men greatly dislike the question "Are you okay?" because it implies they're not. For a woman, too much silence means something's wrong. So if her husband is being quiet for a long period, she may well be concerned. But to be constantly asked if he's okay becomes irritating and wearying to a man. Just assume all is well unless he lets you know otherwise.

  If you can tell something's definitely wrong or he's upset, at least ask, "Is *everything* okay?" rather than, "Are *you* okay?" This tiny adjustment takes away the suggestion that something's wrong with him and puts the emphasis on his circumstances instead. He won't feel as defensive. If he says, "Everything's fine. Why do you ask?" you can answer, "Because I love you and want to make sure all is well in your world." This is a far better response—and far less likely to start an argument—than, "Well, you're just so quiet I thought something was wrong." This last statement puts him into a defensive mode; the first statement does not.

Takeaway: Allow your husband his quietness.

- When you're sad, your husband feels responsible. When he married you, he made the commitment to take care of you—physically, spiritually, and emotionally. When you're down or feeling blue, he often doesn't know what to do, but your mood makes him feel bad, as if he's not doing his job as a man. He sees himself as the warrior, and he sees you as the damsel. A damsel's unhappiness makes the warrior feel incompetent.

  So, if you feel the blues coming on, let him know that you sense them headed your way and that they have nothing to do with him. If he asks what he can do to help, tell him. He can hold you in his arms, or sit beside you as you both read the paper, or take a walk with you. But keep your requests fairly short and doable; make sure it's something within his power to accomplish. For instance, it makes no sense to request that he get your mother and your sister to make up from the big fight they had last week. This is far beyond his control. You could ask him, though, to simply hold you tight for a minute and assure you everything is okay. He can do this…if he's told.

Takeaway: Your sadness impacts your husband more than you may know.

- Men see themselves as helpful, not critical. Again, he's the warrior, and warriors love to assist their damsels. If you feel he's being critical, he probably doesn't see it that way at all. Listen carefully to his words, and then ask yourself if they hold any truth. They probably do. Then take whatever truth they hold and move forward.

Just last night I (Connie) had to run a quick errand. When I got home, Wes had taken a pile of my things I'd scattered on the island in the kitchen and placed them in a large bowl. He then set the bowl on my desk. (He likes the island clean, while I don't mind it rather "busy," especially with my stuff.) He wasn't being critical of my mess at all; he was simply trying to help. My first thought was, *Please don't touch my stuff. If it bothers you, ask me to clean it up and I will.* However, I could tell from his countenance that he really was trying to be helpful—and he was even feeling good about his efforts! He had no idea my mind was brewing with anything other than thankfulness. So why would I make a big deal out of this?

I thanked him for gathering up my stuff and told him how wonderful the counter looked—and it did. Plus, my response kept any tension at bay.

On a related note, let me mention that men don't

like false accusations. (Who does?) To have accused Wes of anything would have been foolish, because his motive was to help. So look for your husband's true motive even if his actions don't match what you wanted done.

Takeaway: Men often "help" in ways we don't always see.

- Men get angry when they feel disrespected or rejected just as women cry when they feel hurt or rejected. It's just how men and women are wired—and this insight is huge!

  We live in a culture that says it's okay for a woman to cry, but it's not okay for a man to become angry—especially with his wife. (We're talking about anger that's expressed appropriately here, by the way—not punching a fist through a wall or screaming expletives at you or the kids.) So don't lecture your husband about his anger without recognizing that it's the twin to your tears. Realize that his testosterone is speaking through his anger just as the estrogen in you is speaking when you cry tears of hurt.

  Takeaway: Don't hold your husband's occasional anger against him.

- Women value relationships; men value accomplishments. That's why "I love you" are the three magic words for a woman, but "I'm so proud of you" are the magic words for a guy.

Takeaway: Let your husband know how proud you are of him.

- If a woman has a fight or an argument with her husband, he may well forget about it during the day. Many women don't; it's never far from their minds. But most men compartmentalize—even the huge fights. This male-female difference has never ceased to amaze us. We think this is one area where we need to change.

    Takeaway: Let go of things quickly.

- Men generally listen more to men than to women. Research proves that this is more than just our female perception. Men actually don't listen to women in the same way they listen to men.

    A recent study by an Italian research group demonstrated that men have a more difficult time processing information from a woman. Male listeners are more likely to *look* at the woman than listen to her and retain the information being relayed.

    The study involved an analysis of men watching news broadcasts. When the reporter was a woman, the men who watched tended to remember her hair color, her approximate age, and whether she was pretty or plain, but they had problems remembering the subject of her report. But when the reporter was male, the men watching remembered far more of the content he reported.

The study also concluded that men are better at processing male voices, and the research revealed an actual disinclination in men to focus on the female voice. None of the men had previously been aware of this, indicating that this occurs on a subconscious level.

Takeaway: A woman is female and a man is male—each has inherently different wiring.

BOTTOM LINE

So much to learn...so little time!

38

CPR for a Dying Marriage

WE HAVE A FRIEND WHOSE HUSBAND recently suffered a massive heart attack and a stroke. When she found him collapsed, she thought at first he was teasing her, since they were planning to go out that evening to celebrate their anniversary. When he didn't respond at all and started to turn blue, she began CPR. She held his nose and breathed into his mouth. She vigorously and repeatedly applied pressure to his chest. And she managed to make an emergency call to 911. She was told to keep up the pressure on his chest even if she broke one of his ribs.

That was three weeks ago. Yesterday I went to see them. He'll need rehab and tender care—but he's alive!

Is your marriage dying or nearly dead?

Let us serve as your 911 operator and suggest some CPR-type steps you can take—with God's guidance and by His power—to put life back into your marriage. The easiest way to get started is something we call blastoff and reentry. Just as these are the two most critical periods in the voyage of a spacecraft, they're also critical moments in your home each day.

Blastoff occurs when the two of you say good-bye to each other in the morning. A dozen other things are probably going on in your home as this happens, but mornings are the perfect time to make sure your husband doesn't feel lonely.

Here are some practical things you can do for your man:

- Get up before him and spend a few moments with God.
- If he drinks coffee, make it and take a cup to him.
- If he likes to peruse the headlines, bring him the newspaper.
- Ask about what lies ahead in his day and how you can be praying for him—and be sure to pray.
- Walk him to the door—or, if you leave before he does, find him—and embrace him.
- Tell him that you love him…and wish him a wonderful day.

And here are some practical preparations for reentry in the evenings:

- Tidy up the house. Just a fast pickup works wonders.
- Men love coming home to a peaceful home. Is yours that?
- Freshen up! Yes, this sounds old fashioned, but it's so true.

- Have a plan for dinner. So many men these days seem to be on their own for meals. Preparing a simple dinner makes him feel treasured. If need be, stop for takeout, but serve it on your dishes rather than in the restaurant containers.

- When he arrives home, stop what you're doing and greet him warmly. If his hands are full, help him. If he gets home before you do, find him.

- Embrace him warmly. Smile! Be happy to see him.

- Get him his favorite beverage, then allow him some chill-out time.

- Tell him you've missed him and are glad he's home.

These ideas for blastoff and reentry may seem simplistic, but their impact on a man can be huge. You see, these actions will show him your love, respect, and esteem. They will speak volumes to your guy about what he means to you. And every guy we know of likes to listen to a woman who's "saying" those things.

BOTTOM LINE

Make mornings and evenings a time
your husband looks forward to.

39

It Won't Always Make Sense

Very early one morning not long ago, I (Connie) was driving downtown with my husband and daughter. It was still dark outside. Wes came to an intersection, and the light was green. He quickened his speed since we were running late.

Out of the corner of my eye, I saw a car going the wrong way on a one-way street that intersected the road we were on—and it was headed straight for us! In the car was an elderly couple who had no idea they were going the wrong way. Of course, they had no traffic light to warn them that they needed to stop.

I screamed, "Stop!" at the top of my lungs. Wes looked at me as if I'd lost my mind, and he let up on the gas a bit. He did a quick check to make sure he'd seen the green light correctly—which he had—and then continued into the intersection. He hadn't noticed the car headed toward us.

As I yelled, "Stop!" again, I reached over to grab the wheel. Wes slammed on the brakes. He still hadn't seen the car, but he'd heard something in my voice that told him he needed to stop.

A split second later the elderly couple passed in front of our stopped car, apparently oblivious to what had almost happened. I believe that if Wes hadn't stopped, someone would have been killed—and it probably would have been Wes, because it was his side of the car that was exposed.

When I yelled, "Stop!" to Wes, that instruction didn't make any sense to him, so he kept going. When I yelled it again, the instruction still didn't make sense to him, but he trusted me enough to stop the car. The urgency in my voice had trumped the green light.

This scene is analogous to how life often is: God tells us to do something His way, but it makes no sense to us. Surely He can't mean we're to respect our husbands if they aren't doing a good job of leading our families. Right? Wrong.

Or surely He doesn't mean we're to be gentle spirited when they're being blunt, direct, and maybe even rude. Right? Wrong.

You see, what our husbands are doing has little to do with what God calls us to do. They may be going down a one-way street in the wrong direction, but that matter is between them and God. Our responsibility is to do what God tells us to do whether or not we understand it and regardless of our feelings on the matter. This assignment isn't easy, and it flies against everything our society tells us to do.

Wrecks happen on the road every day because someone is going the wrong way. People are killed or injured. Wrecks are happening in marriages every day too. To avoid such accidents, we need to listen to God's voice and act accordingly. It may well make sense to you to continue heading through the intersection when the light is green. But if it's not safe—that is, if you're not doing something else God says for you to do—it doesn't matter if the light you see is green. You need to stop, reevaluate the way you're living, and then proceed cautiously.

You can trust that God's way will eventually make sense, even when another way at first seems better...or more fun...or more satisfying. Satan's tactic is to get you focused on yourself, but self-focus is never the right road. You stay on track by listening to God's Word and doing what it says.

We challenge you—even as we challenge ourselves—to stay in God's Word. Do what it says whether or not His instruction makes sense to you and whether or not you feel like it. As you walk in His light, He'll shine more and more light onto the path you're walking. That's just the way He works.

BOTTOM LINE

*God's Word trumps everything—
even the world's green lights.*

AFTERTHOUGHTS

IN THE SUMMER OF 2006, we attended the wedding of a wonderful couple. They recited their vows, promising before God and man that they would love each other no matter what. They exchanged rings, kissed, smiled, jumped for joy, and squealed with happiness (we heard the squeals moments after they'd left the sanctuary).

Jess was unabashedly dizzy with love for Ben, and he for her. During the reception, Ben leaned forward to listen to Jess every time she opened her mouth. They danced and whispered back and forth. Her happiness and his delight were so refreshing to see.

We're reminded in Genesis of the importance of words. God spoke the words, "Let there be light," over that which was formless, void, and dark. And there was light, waters, dry land, vegetation, plants, fruit trees, day, night, stars, heavens, water creatures, birds, sea monsters, every living creature that moves, cattle, creeping things, beasts of the earth. All came into being by the spoken word of God. "So God created man in his own image, in the image of God he created him; male and female he created them." (He fashioned woman from the rib of Adam.) And God brought Eve to Adam, and they became husband and wife.

It will be so exciting to see this young couple living out their covenant to each other and to God. But will Ben keep listening to Jess? Will Jess keep communication open for Ben?

Does your husband continue to want to listen to you? Are you still thrilled to see him at the end of the day? Does he know he's more important to you than your children? your career? your hobbies? your parents? you?

As we were leaving the reception, Ben came running up to say good-bye. Someone asked him, "How's your wife doing?" He stared at us blankly for a moment and then said, "My wife! My wife! *I have a wife!*"

Do you think that's how your husband feels about you? Are you ready to launch out in a whole new direction? Why not set out today?

BOTTOM LINE

It's never too late to start
acting like a newlywed again.

EPILOGUE

WE RECENTLY HEARD A WOMAN talking about her divorce. She was on a panel of women who were discussing what kinds of guys made good marriage partners. This woman said she distinctly remembers that she was breast-feeding her baby when she decided to divorce her husband.

Another woman on the panel asked her, "Didn't it occur to you to try again rather than get divorced?"

The woman replied that she had already "tried again." She said she and her husband had started over a number of times—at least ten.

I (Connie) thought to myself that if I'd divorced Wes after our tenth start-over, we would have been divorced within the first year of our marriage. And I'm being completely serious.

At some point, however, the start-over "took," and what we have today is more precious to me than silver or gold. In fact, Wes said to me just this morning, as the writing of this book was drawing to a close, "I feel closer to you today than I ever have before." God works in strange and wonderful ways.

So, if you're thinking of leaving your husband, we implore you to think again. (If you're being abused or if adultery is involved, you need to seek help *now* and protect yourself and your children.) God Himself created marriage, and marriage is sacred. You don't throw it out simply because you're in a funk or you don't see eye to eye on certain things. If you're unhappy in your marriage, we challenge you to start fresh, following God's principles for you as a wife.

We'd like to close by sharing a tragic story about a friend of ours. One morning she was hustling her kids off to school and her husband off to work. She was slapping peanut butter and jelly sandwiches together for their lunches when her husband blew through the kitchen on his way out the door to go to work. He reached out to kiss her, and she stuck out her neck to receive that kiss as she finished the kids' sandwiches. She said his kiss landed somewhere on the back of her neck. He walked out to the garage, jumped in his car, and headed to work.

Shortly afterward, her phone rang and a voice on the other end told her that her husband had been in a bad car wreck. She would soon learn that her husband had died instantly when an oncoming car hit his truck.

Our friend has thought often about that last, hurried kiss. "How I wish I'd set down that knife, stopped what I was doing, turned, and given him my full attention," she says today. "How I wish I had taken his face in my hands, kissed him, and told him how much I loved him. I would give anything to have that morning back, to have one more moment with him."

The next time you see your husband, do what our friend wishes she'd done that morning. Then do it again the next time you see him. And the next. And the next.

You'll never, ever regret that you did.

———

This has been a difficult week as we come to the close of this book. Ray, Nancy's husband, passed away four days ago, and his funeral was yesterday. The day Ray died, I (Connie) was in Oklahoma to attend the funeral of another dear friend. Meanwhile, three days ago brought the death of the husband of another friend—the woman I mentioned earlier who'd given her husband CPR. His funeral is tomorrow.

Two of Nancy's daughters and their families are staying with us in our home. It has been delightful getting to know them better. They're off doing other things right now. Wes is at work. One of my daughters is baby-sitting, another is at school completing finals, and the third is flying home tonight from college for Christmas vacation.

As I sit in the quiet of my home and reflect, I can't help but think about how quickly time passes and how one day life will come to an end for each of us. This day will come much more quickly than we can ever imagine.

I'm also thinking back to a week ago when we visited Ray in the hospital. It was late at night, and Wes and I had just flown in from Denver. We went by, certain he would be asleep, but wanting to see him just the same. We knew he was gravely ill and his time was very limited.

When we got to his room, he was awake, but it was obvious how sick he was. As he lay on his back with his eyes half-closed, he reached upward with his hand, trying to find Wes's hand. Wes slipped his hand into Ray's, and we sat beside him for a little while. Ray and Wes held hands, and Wes rubbed Ray's tummy with his free one. As you know from reading this book, Ray is a man's man. He's rough and rugged. The world always seemed a safer place knowing he was in it. He's that kind of man.

But as the days—really, the minutes—wound down on his life, the one thing Ray kept repeating to Wes and me was, "I love you. I love you. I love you." In fact, those were his last three words to Nancy before he slipped into the coma from which he would never return.

As I sit here and think about all this, I wonder what it will take for us to get ourselves together and become the wives God intends us to become. We've got to stop waiting on our husbands to change before we do. We have no control over them, but we can choose to change ourselves.

This isn't meant as a chastisement at all—it's meant as a heartfelt cry to everyone reading this book. It's meant as a heartfelt cry for myself especially.

One day, it may well be you or me sitting at the bedside of our dying husband. What will be running through our minds then, when it's too late to start over one more time? Will we be at peace with the way we've treated our men? Will they be able to look into our eyes and know how much we love them and how proud of them we are?

Cold, hostile moments have a way of turning into cold, hostile years—and into cold, wasted lives. How sad it would be to get to the end of one's life and feel only regret about the way you treated the man God entrusted to you so many years before, when you uttered those words: "for better for worse, for richer for poorer, in sickness and in health, to love and to cherish, forsaking all others, till death do us part…"

Right now, will you consider starting over if you need to? before it's too late? while there's still time to invest in your husband's life?

There was a time in Nancy's life where she was angry with Ray more often than she wasn't, yet there came a day when she chose to start over. Having worked closely with Nancy for more than ten years, I'm a witness to her marriage. And I can tell you one thing: I saw in Nancy a woman who loved her husband with everything that was in her. No, he wasn't perfect, nor was she. But she started afresh day after day. And at the end of Ray's life, as he lay in that hospital room, he knew he was deeply loved and admired by the woman sitting at his side. Surely, that knowledge must have given him more peace than any medicine administered by the doctors or nurses.

Now, for you, I close with a simple prayer. Please know that you're being prayed for right this second, as my fingers type out these final few sentences, on this December day in Omaha, Nebraska:

> Dear God, I come humbly before You, knowing You welcome me with open arms. Thank You that I don't have to clean myself up first. Thank You that You welcome me just as I am...every single time I turn to You.
>
> Lord, please give each woman reading this book the strength and the grace—and the desire—to start afresh in her marriage. Please help her accept her husband as he is. Please help her to respect him...to forgive the hurt he may have caused her...to love him and admire him.
>
> Jesus, we know You can do anything. We know You can do far more than we can begin to ask or imagine. So please do it, Lord. Do it now. Would You work a miracle across this nation? Would You work a miracle in our hearts? Would You make us wives who delight Your heart?
>
> Lord, I ask You to warm the heart of every woman reading this book. Help her treat her husband as she

would treat You personally. We know You consider this no small thing. And we know that we can do nothing of lasting value apart from You…and the good news is that we don't have to. Help us never forget that You're just a prayer away…a thought away…a cry away. You're always here. Always.

Thank You in advance, Lord, for all You're going to do in the marriage of each woman reading this book. To You be the honor and glory forever.

Thank you, dear friend, for reading our book. May God bless you richly. And may Ray's legacy to Wes and me also be his legacy to you. Say "I love you" to those you love, and say it over and over and over again. May you never stop saying it—especially to your husband—until death do you part.

ACKNOWLEDGMENTS

THANK YOU TO THOSE of you who prayed this book into fruition. You did every bit as much as our keyboards did. The storms of life were whirling around both of us throughout most of the writing. Your faithful, fervent prayers were felt deeply, and we can't thank you enough.

To Multnomah Books and Random House, thank you for continuing to believe in us and partner with us. We still stand amazed.

To Christine Burkett, words cannot say enough. You know what you did, and we're forever grateful. You're a priceless treasure, and we love you.

To our dear families and sweet friends, thank you for making the tapestry of our lives so rich.

Most of all, to God alone be the glory. Forever and ever and ever.